Endorsements

In *Passing the Peace: A New Paradigm for Christian Community*, Dr. Chet Gean writes from his lifelong experience within the parish, not as a theoretician observing from a distance but as an insider, viewing the challenges and opportunities before Christian congregations. He effectively weaves into his work the observations and insights of mentors like Waetjen, Nouwen, and Buechner, some of the most important religious thinkers in the past century. Chet's clear prose is enhanced as well by striking photography and excerpts from his previously published volumes of poems. This book is an important addition to the pastor's tool kit.

—**Rev. Dave Brown**
Immanuel Presbyterian Church, Tacoma, WA

In this age of secularization, as Christians begin to move out of a culture of consumerism, instantism, and the growing meaninglessness of life and enter into a culture of authenticity, Dr. Gean's book opens a new paradigm for pastoral ministry. [Through it,] he draws both church leadership and laity into a more immediate spirituality of living in God's presence. Tom Ehrich's seven areas of community care are examined in the light of Gean's own experiences in parish ministry. [In this book,] written out of his experiences of many years in the ministry, Gean discloses his love, respect, and solicitude for the church and summons it to identify itself with this hunger for authenticity in faith and discipleship.

At the heart of this new paradigm is the repetition of incarnation, God's incarnation in Jesus Christ repeated in the life of everyone who submits to the invitation that Jesus issues to those who would be his disciples: "Come and see!" Crossing the bridge into a spirituality of authenticity, so that the Word will become flesh in our own time and place, requires an open-eyed faith that sees the world as it is in all of its hatred and injustice and yet believes that by engaging [it] in a discipleship that is empowered by God's indwelling Spirit, the world in all of its evil will be transformed. Gean accentuates imagination in this paradigm of spirituality, offers poetry (his own and that of others), and features stunning photography by Stan McMeekin to inspire creativity and promote the individual expression of imagination in order to enrich and rejuvenate the community of faith in its continued fellowship. Entering the Body of Christ through baptism and engaging in spiritual discipline in everyday life by combining reflection and prayer with Scripture reading and regular participation in the Eucharist will begin to actualize the long-overlooked paradigm of incarnation that Jesus inaugurated.

—**Herman C. Waetjen**
Robert S. Dollar, Emeritus Professor of New Testament
San Francisco Theological Seminary

Passing the Peace held my interest—start to finish! This book has much to say to pastors, non-ordained staff, and lay teachers. The poetry strengthens the book.

—**Paul Middents**, Captain
USN (Retired)

Chet Gean's treatise on evil identifies the negative energy that is at play in our families and communities—grudges, anger, jealousy, victim mentalities, narcissism, refusal to forgive, vindictiveness, selfishness, entitlement, and the list goes on. In today's culture, relationships are often seen as disposable if they cause discomfort or stress or require adapting or growing in tolerance. Acknowledging our own brokenness and need for grace will promote healing, restore relationships, and invite peace into our lives. You will be enriched and enlightened by reading this book.

—**Carol Olsen**
Gig Harbor Press

I felt privileged and enriched by reading *Pass the Peace: A New Paradigm for Christian Community*. I felt a new sense of love and mystery. It flowed and engaged me in the process. On many occasions, I felt an "Aha!" experience, when things I had not articulated for myself seemed to fit into the mosaic of my spiritual journey. I hope pastors who wrestle with tides of love and eddies of evil will be enriched and encouraged to keep the tiller and steer the ferry as it gathers those willing to journey together.

—**Robert Dick**, Attorney

Pass the Peace

A New Paradigm for Christian Community

DR. CHET B. GEAN, D.MIN.

CAROL OLSEN, M.A., CONTRIBUTING EDITOR

STAN MCMEEKIN, PHOTOGRAPHY

Photography: Stan McMeekin; Solana Productions NW

WinePress Publishing (PO Box 428, Enumclaw, WA 98022) functions only as book publisher. As such, the ultimate design, content, editorial accuracy, and views expressed or implied in this work are those of the author.

Unless otherwise noted, all Scriptures are taken from the *New Revised Standard Version Bible*: Anglicized Edition, copyright 1989, 1995, Division of Christian Education of the National Council of the Churches of Christ in the United States of America. Used by permission. All rights reserved.

Where noted, quotes are from *The Message*, copyright © 1993, 1994, 1995, 1996, 2000, 2001, 2002, Hardback Edition. Used by permission of Navpress Publishing Group. The views expressed in this book are solely those of the author and do not necessarily reflect the views of the publisher, and the publisher thereby disclaims any responsibility for them.

Scripture references marked RSV are taken from the *Revised Standard Version* of the Bible. © 1946, 1952, 1971 by the Division of Christian Education of the National Council of the Churches of Christ in the U.S.A. Used by permission.

ISBN 13: 978-1-4141-2308-0
ISBN 10: 1-4141-2308-6
Library of Congress Catalog Card Number: 2012902486

Theology, with all its power and substance, must return to the
parish in ways that can be understood by the community.

—Chet Gean

To my wife, Arline, whose constant
support and love kept me going in body
and spirit, renewing my energy
for the journey, encouraging and enabling
me to complete this work

I Am a Country Boy

I am a country boy who grew up poor
I am a late bloomer given the chance
To do a work late in life
With the same energy as before
But with more measured and thoughtful intent
I am a listener to the inner world
In its darkness and light
I am a country boy whose teachers valued
Baying hounds in the night
Teachers like Audrey who taught us about God and
The purpose of life
Teachers who bridged their thoughts
And deeds
Teachers who lived life as they taught
I am a country boy who went to war in faraway places
I learned the mundane, the meanness,
And the evil of war
I learned to be God's man, learned to understand
The faulted and sinful parts
Learned the blessed and loved parts too

I learned to prepare the way, to clear the paths of His way
So others might know the God of the Way
I am a country boy
Loved and called
To do His work

—Chet Gean ©2011

Contents

Acknowledgments

To my friend and mentor, Richard G. Johnson, M.D. Ph.D., whose courage bridged the medical and religious worlds and helped me find the pathway to the present. His life has always been a source of strength.

To my friend and seminary teacher, Herman C. Waetjen, Professor of New Testament at San Francisco Theological Seminary, who taught us by deed and word. His encouragement and enthusiasm are appreciated. He has enriched my life; it is a pleasure to know him.

To my editor and friend, Carol Olsen. Thank you for the excellent work. She questioned and helped clarify and ultimately smoothed the road to publication. I give my heartfelt appreciation.

To Stan McMeekin, Solana Productions NW, whose photography and intuitive spirit provided the bridge between the worlds often unperceived. I give my deepest gratitude.

To my family and friends, who contributed with comments and suggestions, I salute and smile with thanks: Dave Brown, Paul Middents, Jill Ann Jones, Bob Dick, and others.

Foreword

> We have the awesome responsibility of being able to construct
> our own future and having to choose whether to and how to
> participate in that creative process.
> —Ed Lindaman in his seminal book
> *Thinking in the Future Tense*

In *Pass the Peace: A New Paradigm for Christian Community,* Dr.
Chet Gean gives the community called church a new resource as
it engages in the creative process of constructing its future.

Chet writes from his lifelong experience within the parish, not
as a theoretician observing from a distance but as an insider, viewing
the challenges and opportunities before Christian congregations.
He writes as someone who cares deeply for the health and future
of Christian communities. He effectively weaves into his work
the observations and insights of mentors like Waetjen, Nouwen,
and Buechner, some of the most important religious thinkers in
the past century. Chet's clear prose is enhanced as well by striking
photography and excerpts from his previously published volumes of
poems. This book is an important addition to the pastor's tool kit.

In this book, Chet shows respect for the participants in
congregational life. He respects their ability to think theologically.
His emphasis on thinking theologically is a needed corrective

in a time when entertainment seems to be replacing thoughtful reflection and worship. *Pass the Peace* is hopeful for the Christian future without being naive about the challenges before Christian communities today. This is particularly evident in Chet's thoughtful discussion of the reality of evil, especially in its institutional forms. As Christians are experiencing increased conflict within their tradition, Chet recognizes that conflict is real. He holds out the idea that we can disagree without being abusive and express opposing views without losing the ability to be civil.

The author of *Pass the Peace* is comfortable with paradoxes. Chet has the remarkable ability to think analytically while leaving open space for mystery and the *sacred hunch*. He calls on church leaders to trust their intuition and for lay people to claim their rightful place in the community called *church*.

Pass the Peace is a labor of love. It is a gift and a useful tool for those engaged in constructing the future of the beloved community.
—**Rev. Dave Brown**
Immanuel Presbyterian Church, Tacoma, WA

Introduction

"The Parable of the Good Coach"

It was New Year's Day. Two teams prepared for the big game: one from the east and one from the west. The teams' records were equally matched, and the bleachers shook as fans expressed their enthusiasm. The teams faced off from their respective benches on opposite sides of the field.

The coaches were seasoned and their records exemplary. They assumed their opposing positions in equally opposing styles. The coach from the east sat in a seat high above the field, physically removed from his team. He stared down at the field, arms crossed, wearing a stoic expression. Distant and uninvolved, his body language discouraged engagement. He spoke only to deny an interview from a news reporter and waved off an approaching cameraman.

In contrast, a flurry of activity surrounded the coach on the west side of the playing field. Filled with joy and excitement, he delivered final words of encouragement to his team, exchanged high fives, bumped shoulders with fists, waved in response to shouts from fans, and answered a myriad of questions posed by curious reporters.

The team from the west burst onto the field, a picture of pride, youth, and strength. United by resolve and bound together by the color of their uniforms, the players anticipated the upcoming struggle.

In primal red and black uniforms, the team circled up and began a ceremonial dance. "It's our day; we can do anything," the men grunted and chanted as their arms went around each other to form a chain hug. Moving as one organism, they drew the circle in tight, melding their strength and spirit. Then with a "Whoop!" they broke out, shouting, "Let's get 'em! This one's ours! Whoo-hoo!" The dance was followed by a loosely choreographed display of chest bumps, hugs, hip slapping, and high tens.

Meanwhile, suited up in black and gold, the players from the east stood in silence, sporting blank stares—not sure what to make of this exuberant team from the west.

The referee flipped a coin to determine who would kick and who would receive. The west won the right to receive. The east kicked the ball, which was picked up at the ten yard line and carried to the fifteen. The west moved carefully, waiting for their secret rhythm to show itself, and then it began; over and over the magic repeated. They made their way down the field one play at a time: a run here, a short pass there, a first down, a long pass, a touchdown, a thwarted field goal, an interception, another touchdown. The winning streak continued. It was not the equally matched game the fans anticipated, since the score at halftime was 35-0.

As the teams returned for the second half of play, the team from the east appeared determined to turn things around. In charge of the ball, the offense moved it down the field ten yards at a time. Deep in the end zone, the east made a final push for their first touchdown of the game. Their supporters stood, waving and screaming.

"Don't get mad! Just get better," the coach from the west hollered to his team.

The second and third quarters were touch and go as the teams pushed each other forward and back, gaining and losing acquired turf. Then, in the final minutes of the fourth quarter, the east sacked the quarterback and pushed for a second touchdown, making the final score 35-14. The east had come back strong, though not enough to win the game.

The team from the west erupted in cries of victory and celebration. Their coach showed no distress over the poor showing of his team during the second half. He smiled, hugged, and laughed. The outcome had been clear to him all along, and he had met his objective.

What made the difference? Was it strategy, leadership, team involvement, or the dance? Perhaps all of the above played a part. What changed in the second half of play? The answer is simple: the coach from the west sent in his second string team to get experience for the next year.

Invitation from the Author

This is a call to a new style of worship, a new pattern of being together in community. Christ taught through parables, and I have attempted to illustrate my vision for a renewed Christian community in "The Parable of the Good Coach." Old leadership styles are not working in the church. The laity seems aware, but they hesitate to take action until it is too late. The basic infrastructure of the church and its administration has gone unattended. Vital human and economic resources are spent without perception of the health and integrity of the whole. Crisis comes in the way of scandal, disunity, and widespread disillusion with religion. The result is our estrangement from God and from one another.

My years of experience as a pastor, a denominational leader, and a consultant serving churches in crisis have led me to write this book, to share my understandings, and to invite my fellow believers to again find the Way. I will reflect on church management, laity involvement, systems integrity, leadership models, the spiritual practices of the parish, the worship of God, and the energy of Christ in community.

In short, I am proposing a new paradigm for church leadership and laity involvement, one that embraces the mystical energy of God and approaches our parish communities organically, with a deep appreciation for the flow of God's energy in our midst and out into the world we are called to serve. It is a call to experience Christ's Spirit in us, among us, and through us.

This new paradigm welcomes intuition and imagination in worship and encourages the biblically-based practices of dream interpretation, meditation, solitude, and listening for the voice of God in prayer.

I will identify and unmask the evil that is at work in our communities and expose the ways in which religion perpetuates evil through the misuse of power and the distortion of truth.

Together we will explore bridges to worship in the form of music, poetry, drama, and dance; discover ways to enliven the sacraments; and interface worship with the natural wonders of God's creation.

This invitation takes seriously the historical, critical method of biblical interpretation while employing the imagination to make Christ's message pertinent and compelling to a new generation of believers.

I am calling the world to peace, to the mystery of inner healing, to wholeness, and to our God, who alone loves in a manner unique and perfectly suited to each one of us, never resting until we are safely in his embrace. I invite a shift toward grace, a theology of grace, and a journey of grace. It is my hope to push and stretch the sacred mystery to a place beyond words, to grasp more deeply the meaning of Jesus' words as he cried over the woodenness of his generation:

> We played the flute for you,
> And you did not dance;
> We wailed,
> And you did not mourn
> For John came neither eating nor drinking
> And they say, "He has a demon."
> The son of man came eating and drinking and they say,
> "Look a glutton and a drunkard
> A friend of tax collectors and sinners?"
>
> —Matthew 11:16–19

Part 1
Come and See

Chapter 1

Best Practices

God's various ministries are carried out everywhere, but all originating in God's spirit. Each person is given something to do that shows who God is. Everyone gets in on it; everyone benefits. The variety is wonderful.

—*The Message*, page 2083

For the church to thrive and grow, in keeping with Christ's teachings, attention must be paid to the underlying structure and organization of the parish ministry. The Apostle Paul, in his letters to the church in Corinth, explains that Christ's body—the church—is made up of "different-but similar parts arranged and functioning together" (*The Message*, p. 2084). One's personal significance is based on what he or she is a part of. "The way God designed our bodies is a model for understanding our lives together as a church: every part dependent on every other part" (*The Message*, p. 2084).

A portion of my ministry took place in Hollywood, so I am familiar with the film industry promoters' efforts to build excitement for upcoming blockbusters by creating a buzz about each project. Jesus also created a buzz when he asked John the Baptist's disciples, "What are you looking for?" Jesus answered their looks of curiosity with, "Come, and see" (John 1:38).

People are open to and curious about religion because they are looking for another world, one other than the one they have experienced. This is the work, to imagine a world beyond the five senses. The image held by many today is a hunger for a conceptual world, one of community, where all are welcomed and embraced. The modern preacher, burdened by the demands of his profession, is encouraged to move from his own spiritual and private struggles to the Spirit-source of comfort and enlightenment found in Christian community.

The modern church's "Come and see" umbrella covers a broad range of offerings: music and drama, local and international humanitarian missions, recovery support groups, grief counseling, marriage and family counseling, weddings and memorials, and a myriad of social activities for all ages.

What is largely overlooked is that motivated people come to church looking for something. God's Spirit leads them, or someone steers them to the energy of the community. This energy is called the "Holy Presence." The Holy Spirit flows freely in the Christian community. It was a noted hallmark of the early Christian community and continues today. Like electricity seeking a conductor, the Spirit moves among the people, creating the flow of enlightenment. Worshippers catch the spark and pass the Spirit along.

This energy operates on a variety of levels. It moves within the structure of the liturgy, its light touches the creator of music and song, and it empowers sacred words to become *living words*. The words carry content to harness the passion of the leaders' personalities and create a buzz within the community of worshippers.

My course of personal development has revolved around listening to worship experts who are trying to bring sense to liturgy and structure to our sacred places. Some provide excellent insights, while others miss the mark profoundly. Most of the current focus tends to center around the style of the music or preaching. The issues, however, go beyond contemporary styles versus traditional forms, or the kinds of music being sung. The issues are the content of the message—spoken or sung—excellence of delivery, and the energy of God that enters the realm of sacred trust.

Tom Ehrich, who is a church consultant, an Episcopal priest, and the author of *Church Wellness: A Best Practices Guide to Nurturing Healthy Congregations*, argues convincingly that the focus of healthy religious communities lies in deploying best practices in community care. He puts forth an organic view of religious community, delineating best practices in seven areas:

1. Personal Development—invitation, excitement, challenge, enablement, and involvement
2. Leadership—call, train, support, encourage
3. Communication Strategy—message, strategy, and content
4. Spiritual Development—basics of the Book, prayer and meditation, the Sacraments, and friends in community
5. Youth—create, engage, and stimulate children, young adults, and young families
6. Listening to Needs—model compassion, and develop trust and worthy responses to the community and the world
7. Evaluation—consistent, measurable, and results-driven

I will examine these seven elements in light of my own experiences as a parish minister and as a consultant working with churches in crisis.

Personal Development

It is not enough for folks to show up for church on Sunday and call it good. If the church is to be more than a drive-by experience, its membership must be educated and spiritual disciplines practiced. Only then can the parish become a vital, healthy community.

For the Protestant church, spiritual discipline comes first in the Holy Scripture and the Good News as it is proclaimed. Nothing is more important. Reflection, prayer, and insight stem from our sacred text, the Bible. With that being said, it has taken a Catholic priest by the name of Henri Nouwen to remind the Protestant world of the discipline of the heart and the discipline of the church.

Discipline of the heart, described by Nouwen in *The Only Necessary Thing*, is to create a context in which the life of uninterrupted prayers and service can develop (p. 1). For Nouwen, the discipline of the heart calls for setting aside time each day to be in the presence of God and to listen with open hands. It is to recognize the limitation of being human, to discover that "all of our strength, hope, courage, and confidence" may best be found in God's presence (p. 93). It is to recognize that the discipline of the heart requires daily reflection to nurture the mind and enable contemplation and meditation.

Imagination is central to Nouwen's inductive method. Thus, Christ is not limited to his time and culture but bridges the centuries to be seen, heard, touched, and engaged through imagination. Christ is then a living presence with whom we can enter into deep conversations in the present (p. 101).

A Sunday Prayer

The sounds of the ocean
Distant and close;
The sounds of God
In silence begin the day.
How does one pray
Without a stumbling, hesitant word?
It is not easy to say,
"I have need of you"
When silence is so strong
"Come let us reason together,"
The Psalmist wrote,

And we utter the words
Although we wonder as we speak,
What will he say?
Come, shepherd of the past,
Come shepherd of our silence;
Come friend of friendship,
Of inner sight
Speak, console, hear
Our utterances.
Can words touch
Feelings describe
The spirit hear
What I cannot say?

—**Chet B. Gean**
from *Thoughts in Time* ©2003

The discipline of the church, in simplest terms, is the standard for the community of God's people. Creating a community that approaches God's standards, however, is neither simple nor possible without God's help. It is a complex, living mosaic, a tapestry of gains and losses, joys and sorrows, ups and downs, steps and missteps (p. 124). St. Peter describes the church as being composed of "living stones" crafted together into community. Each stone, insignificant in itself, is joined together, resulting in a mosaic that portrays the face of Christ, making visible God in the world (1 Peter 2:4–10).

The community creates a sense of belonging, a family of God. However, as with our biological families, togetherness also exposes our estrangements, our disconnection from our deepest selves, one another, our world, and God. In the simplest terms, community is a wonderful thing; yet, in its complexity, there is always a potential for conflict. The resulting tension is a continuous and humbling reminder of Christ's expectation, his intention for his church. Nouwen explains:

We are together, but we cannot fulfill each other. We can help each other, but we also have to remind each other that our destiny is beyond our togetherness. It is not enough to say that a new relationship with Christ leads to a new relationship with each other. Rather, we must say that the mind of Christ is the mind that gathers us together in community; our life in community is the manifestation of the mind of Christ. (p. 125–128)

What may be at stake within community discipline is the use of the biblical Word as it guides and instructs community life. The Bible is to be used as a discipline and the source of inspiration. The often-quoted passage in Isaiah 40:1–2, "Comfort, O Comfort my people, says your God. Speak tenderly to Jerusalem, and cry to her, that she has served her term, that her penalty is paid, that she has received from the Lord's hand double for all her sins," are words that not only guide the individual but also are a hallmark promise for the church community. Familiar quotes, routinely and frequently delivered, can be empowered by imagination to kindle intuition. The remainder of Isaiah 40 is filled with dramatic images of God's forgiveness, care, and desires for his people as paraphrased in *The Message*:

> The creator of all you can see or imagine has scooped up the ocean in his two hands, measured the sky between his thumb and little finger, has put all the earth's dirt in one of his baskets, and weighed each mountain and hill. Who could ever have told God what to do? What expert would he have gone to for advice; what school would he attend to learn justice? Have you not been paying attention? Have you not been listening? God doesn't come and go. God lasts. He's creator of all you can see or imagine. He doesn't get tired out, doesn't pause to catch his breath. He energizes those who get tired but those who wait upon God get fresh strength. They spread their wings and soar like eagles. They run and don't get tired; they walk and don't lag behind. (p. 1283–1284)

Most clergy have been trained in historical criticism and taught to keep the text in its timely context and recover its meaning from the author. That being said, one cannot go far as a reader or teacher without enlivening the text with imagination and making application to life today. In short, the inductive listening of the heart, the soul, and every corner of our bodies, conscious and unconscious, dreams and visions, all come together as we read or listen to the text. This sort of inductive listening may be the most clearly defined paradigm shift in the new humanity and will most assuredly promote Jesus' Spirit in the sons and daughters of God.

Walter Brueggemann confirms what every good preacher learns as he faces the text privately in meditation and in the context of sermon preparation: that in order to be pertinent and compelling, and to bring the text alive, imagination is required. Preparation is vital. Yet, at times, the inspiration is revealed only in the act of delivery. It troubles the minds of some orderly process thinkers to experience the unexpected. But the poet and the storyteller know the power of the innovative play of words or the unexpected twist in plot. Imagination unfolds with such power that folks are touched and healed.

My associate, David, and I did something "off the cuff" every Sunday before worship. We called this exercise the "Hot Potato." We used it at the opening of the service to get the congregation's attention. David was fast on his feet. I was the straight man. We played against each other with one-liners. The congregation loved it. I sometimes walked in with a golf club as a prop. If my point was a tough one, I would give him a heads-up. Either way, he rarely missed; he had a great sense of balance. It was a pleasure to work with him, and it truly grieved me when he moved on to his own parish. He is still there, and I know why: he helps people to laugh as he pushes the text into real life. He is an example of living out the gift of imagination.

The disciplines of prayer and meditation are two of the most difficult and ignored practices in the church community. No doubt it is because prayer and meditation require privacy and quiet. The chattering mind has a need to slow down; journaling is very helpful in this process. The Psalmist's words "Be still and know I am God!" (46:10) keep reminding one who meditates that everything needs to be disclosed: fear, passions, failures, needs, and impossible situations. Being quiet takes time and a willingness to allow the mind to meander, to zigzag about. In the middle of meditation, something usually occurs—a conversation, a dialogue, or a cry of pain. In the midst of a petition, a smile breaks through or an insight intrudes. Prayers and poems may speed over a lump in the throat or appear to float like music in the air. But nothing is simple or straightforward, because meditation is centered in the right side of the brain, where the unconscious breaks forth—irresistible and, at times, terrifying. Prayer is the center of this creativity, and its power is never to be underestimated. It is God's gift, and its daily application represents a paradigm shift, a powerful tonic for the drama of daily living.

The sacrament of infant baptism begins and ends in mystery. A child is birthed, then baptized. In covenant tradition, it is an agreement among God, the parents, and the parish. It is a beautiful event. The parents understand the promises made at one level, while the parish senses another, and perhaps God yet another. Each participant promises to help bring the child into awareness of God as the source of all love. It is a kind of circle that operates despite a family moving from one city to another, despite the difficulty of spirituality within us, and despite the challenges of providing continuing Christian education. Most importantly, the community identifies and supports the commitments made as best they can.

Emotions may run deep at such times, and the mystery of God may show itself or observe from the shadows. My father was a son of a Methodist minister. No doubt he was baptized as a boy. Like a lot of preachers' kids, he was brought up in the *manse*, or parsonage, of the rural churches of those days. My grandfather was independent and tough, making growing up difficult for my dad at times. When I was young, my dad flatly refused to attend church. I sensed that was not unusual, so I never blamed Dad, even though I didn't understand his reluctance. My mother, on the other hand, was faithful and saw to it that all three of her children attended worship.

In his later years, my father had a stroke. The stroke disabled him, keeping him from putting words together. I made a great effort to understand him as he tried to talk. In our efforts to communicate, a strange thing happened. I began to figure out or intuit what he was thinking. One day, after a lot of efforts back and forth to understand one another, I sensed what was on his mind. He wanted to be baptized; he wanted to join the church.

Well, as soon as we could arrange it, my father was baptized and received into the membership of the church. To the casual observer, this was a routine event. However, for our family, who had prayed all those years for him, it was a profound and powerful occasion—a covenant-mystery filled with emotion. Sometimes, the sacrament becomes the grace about which we preach. We are left in wonder and amazement at the faithfulness of our God.

The sacrament called the Eucharist represents not only the *body of Christ* in his community but also bears witness to his *new humanity* present in this world. To take the sacramental bread, one acknowledges the living Spirit of Christ within—taking on the new humanity symbolized in the bread. To take the sacramental wine is to commit to follow Christ into the new covenant that the wine represents. Participation is essential, for as the symbol of the bread and the symbol of the wine are taken, one pledges to follow Christ into his ministry. The new humanity within each participant represents the *paradigm shift* into community and ministry. The shift becomes apparent when the Spirit is incarnate within each person and the new humanity follows the footprints of Jesus as he calls intuitively, "Follow me." In short, the community becomes incarnate!

The sacrament is the most divine and the most common of things. For if we face our own brokenness and respond to his call to a compassionate life, the sacrament is then placed where our common brokenness and the life of Christ meet. The walls of achievement, competition, and upward mobility are removed, and we become brothers and sisters in Christ's new humanity. The sacrament represents the incarnate life.

The sacrament represents the incarnation not only of God in Christ but also the incarnation in each person and in Jesus' community. When the indwelling of Christ's Spirit occurs, the inspiration and empowerment to minister becomes a reality. Moreover, the sacrament conveys God's love for us and promotes the process of a new humanity manifested in Jesus' ministry (John 14:16–17, 26).

In stark contrast, the Eucharist has also been an instrument of great division within the church body. The invitation is to God's table, with God in Christ as host, yet many are barred from this dispensation of grace by religious institutions and by both conscious and unconscious gatekeepers. Many words have been written in an attempt to understand the meaning of the Eucharist. I find joy in walking down the aisle to receive the elements. There is something about the *walking* that engages me and connects my spirit with others. I like the feeling that arises in the participation and the acting out. I love to watch the tenderness and kindness reflected on the faces of the people. I expect it has something to do with confession and forgiveness—two deep wells of healing.

The children of God, old and young, fill a variety of categories and outlooks and convictions, but in the simplest sense, the community is a living organism, the *new humanity* in the present. When the people of God worship and pray together, they become a creative force for good. This wonderful Holy Spirit has the potential to heal at deep levels. Unfortunately, dysfunction and disorder at times enter into the community. The children of God become ill (out of sorts), resulting in a spiritual disturbance. If the disorder is ignored, it can threaten the community's life force. In a later chapter, I will address these threats to the community.

It is essential that not only leaders but also all of God's people be trained, empowered, and trusted. Boundaries need to be clearly set. God's power is needed to do the ministry. Judicious and prudent pastors are given the trust to lead, and those who oversee the pastors are granted the power to advise and guide them. There are plenty of trust busters. Barbara Blodgett's recent book, *Lives Entrusted*, makes this point. Broken confidentiality, gossip, and "ecclesiastical B.S." (two-faced behaviors) head her list of trust breakers (p.136).

Executive leaders on the whole tend to be administrative, neglecting the responsibility to be pastoral. There is a breakdown in the system, with leaders giving an impression of non-support to local pastors and communities. The end result of this benign neglect is the breeding of mistrust. Blodgett argues that healthy trust relationships are indispensable to faith communities. Trust, however, cannot be taken for granted or be assumed. To be a healthy and authentic community, trust must be nurtured and maintained.

The community begins in worship of God and continues in ministry. Everyone is a part of the whole. Everyone is there to worship God. Presence meets presence. Spirit meets spirit. Confession meets forgiveness. Gratefulness and solidarity meet the gifts of praise. The community encounters the presence of God. It is a dance, a courtship, an event carefully and deeply felt. Love is exchanged, and wonder is experienced. It is simple, yet equally profound. The tone may be somber or humorous. The Spirit of the community is tangible. It makes room for the newcomer to join in but always with sensitivity so that freedom and integrity may be found. The choice to be a part or not to be a part is recognized.

Leadership

In 1964, Robert R. Blake and Jane Mouton published *The Managerial Grid.* This classic work, now called *The Leadership Grid®*, established a framework for understanding leadership styles. Blake and Mouton described two extreme leadership styles: the leader whose main concern is production and the leader whose primary concern is for the people. The authors concluded that the most effective leader achieves high work performance through leading his people to become dedicated to the organizational goals. A high degree of participation and teamwork satisfies the basic need of people to be involved. This correlates to a greater commitment to their work. The leader who inspires involvement is characterized as open-minded and flexible. This is the style of leadership demonstrated in "The Parable of the Good Coach" and is the one most suited to effective parish life.

Such a leadership style speaks to a needed paradigm shift in the Christian community. Shared leadership between clergy and laity was modeled in the early church. Yet, today, the model has too often become one of top-down management. This authoritarian style has limited the voice of the laity and stifled Spirit-directed creativity. Little has been written about the incarnation and the indwelling of God's Spirit that give inspiration and empowerment for ministry to clergy and laity.

In 1982, Thomas J. Peters and Robert H. Waterman, Jr., wrote *In Search of Excellence: Letters from America's Best-Run Companies*, promoting bottom-up business management. Their model encouraged listening to the customer, fostered innovation, valued employees at all levels, involved leaders in day-to-day operations, encouraged companies to identify and hone in on their core product or specialty, and promoted keeping the administration staff lean while transferring the shared vision and autonomy to those at the "shop level." Their analysis indicated that top-down management by an "Imperial CEO" was no longer effective.

These findings have direct application to the parish. How do you build an organization and community with as much involvement and excellence as possible, while staying true to Christ's vision, meeting a myriad of needs, and challenging spiritual growth?

Today's churches need pastors who are present on the benches, on the field, and in the locker rooms of our lives. We need preacher-mentors with a style that is open and engaging, molding people into discipleship. Since the pastor cannot be in all places at once, responsible, small task forces are the key. Much can be accomplished in small groups larger than two and no larger than twelve. Pastors need to be involved in continuing education, building and adapting their skills, nurturing their own spirituality, and always *walking the talk*.

I have always been convinced that good leaders and disciples are hidden in the parish. They need to be coaxed out of their hiding places, developed, nurtured, challenged, enabled, trusted, and empowered. New people need to be invited to get involved and find a place in the ministry. Newcomers often sit on the sidelines, unless there is a conscious effort to engage them.

My life has been enriched with such hidden mentors: a pastor here, a scholar there, a poet here, and a developer there, a doctor here, and many kind friends there who gave and received. Someone invited another to his circle, a vision was shared, and exciting miracles happened. New leadership was identified and enabled.

Episcopal priest Samuel Shoemaker recognized the hidden wisdom and leadership potential in Bill Wilson, who had received divine inspiration in the form of twelve steps. He assisted Bill in writing *Alcoholics Anonymous*. Sam too had once been a hidden leader and was mentored into effective leadership, giving rise to the *Faith at Work* movement. Both programs were based upon the premise that the church exists to convey to all men and women the message of Christ and to build the kingdom of God on the earth. These leaders were members of the *living kingdom,* where one person enabled another to find God and his own God-given place in ministry.

The body of Christ functions best when it is team focused. Shared leadership is marked by invitations to serve, excitement, challenge, enablement, and involvement. Like a body toned by good diet and exercise, the healthy parish moves with energy and excitement. The dance is gentle, beautiful, warm, and very human. People like each other, and they learn to forgive and be forgiven. Grace is primary. Jesus is primary. The person is primary. Leaders become servants. *Downward mobility,* to use Henri Nouwen's term, is the way of Jesus.

What do grace, Jesus, and the individual person mean in the context of Christ-focused, team leadership? In essence, the participants become God's beloved as Jesus was beloved (Mark 1:11). At Jesus' baptism, God affirmed Jesus' identity by saying, "You are my beloved on whom my favor rests" (Luke 3:21 and John 1:29–34). The term *beloved* embraces all who accept and follow Jesus' life into his new humanity birthed by the Holy Spirit. In simplest terms, God's love empowers the new humanity by being in the person, with the person, and for the person. To be beloved as Jesus was beloved changes the focus from the person to God. Belovedness is a given—God loves without condition. One's existence is not centered in the self but in being beloved by God. Our task then is to simply accept our *belovedness,* to rest in God's love.

The cosmic battle between evil and God lies at the heart of belovedness. Evil represents the absence of love and is in direct opposition to everything incarnate within the beloved. Just as Jesus became incarnate with God's spirit of belovedness, so do his followers. We become agents of belovedness and agents of incarnation. God is *in us, for us,* and *with us.* The paradigm shift in leadership is best exemplified in Jesus' washing the feet of his disciples and his admonition to his followers to live out their incarnation in service.

Thus, a downward-mobility community is based upon servant leader figures and a servant ministry. St. Paul captured the theology of Jesus' thinking in his letters from prison to the church at Philippi. His words are translated in *The Message:*

If being in a community of the Spirit means anything to you, if you have a heart, if you care—then do me a favor. Agree with each other, love each other, be deep-spirited friends. Don't push your way to the front: don't sweet-talk your way to the top. Put yourself aside, and help others get ahead. Don't be obsessed with getting your own advantage. Forget yourselves long enough to lend a helping hand.

—*The Message*, page 2138

Servant mentality requires an emptying of self, a supple willingness to go where God leads. The journey is often difficult. Frequently, the servant ministry is a call not only for leaders and people to go but also an invitation to go where they would rather not go. Sometimes it is a place where the community feels uncomfortable and insecure, a place where one's achievements go unrecognized and no awards are given.

Christ's call to servitude flies in the face of a society moving in the opposite direction. The larger society is focused on upward mobility based on competition, individual achievement, and the survival of the strongest. It is a culture that says, "The animal that walks funny is someone else's lunch. So stay alert! Keep up your pretense and look lively!" When this secular view of leadership is emulated in the church, the result is an uncompassionate church and a mockery of the love Jesus demonstrated in his ministry to the marginalized and his ultimate death on the cross.

The wealthiest churches in the most beautiful communities are positioned to provide the strongest ministries to our world. Instead, many represent a kind of cheap grace that Dietrich Bonheoffer described in his book *The Cost of Discipleship*, when speaking of the German church during the Second World War. The ultimate result is a culture that is not called to repentance and not challenged by God's judgment. Such cultures market a distorted grace, a theology without substance.

Upward mobility is central to the American culture. If the church is not careful, it can end up like the proverbial *tar baby*, caught in a sticky situation, where secular demands compete with the admonition of Jesus "to bring good news to the poor, to proclaim release to those held captive, to give sight to the blind, to let the oppressed go free, and to proclaim the year of the Lord's favor" (Luke 4:18).

How can we balance the mobility issue without getting entangled in conflicting demands? It is complicated, as perspectives differ and perceptions of truth differ. The American culture was built on the dream that hard work, discipline, and a competitive search for the best would create a great society, and it has. But somewhere along the line, we lost our responsibility to the segment of society that could not compete, could not keep up. Wealth, power, and success became our new gods. As corporations gained power, the government became a tool to be manipulated, a well to satisfy corporate thirst, rather than an instrument to serve the needs of people. Blind achievement without balance or a desire to provide a better world for others is a kind of god in modern clothing. Such a culture suggests that envy is good, greed is good, wealth is good, and self is good. It says, "I got mine. Now you go get yours." It is survival focused—hollow and without significant meaning beyond the immediate satisfaction of eating, sleeping, drinking, and amusing oneself. It leads to an expanding, emotional black hole.

A life of *downward mobility*, on the other hand, acknowledges our needs but goes beyond our animal needs for survival; it celebrates the gifts and talents given to us. These gifts are to be used to celebrate life and to fulfill one's destiny, not for oneself but to help and encourage others. It chooses life and not death (Deut. 1:34). It builds others up, it helps and guides others, it enjoys others, it gives a hand to others, and it lives a life of love and compassion. The model is Jesus, whose words and acts and ultimate sacrifice of love ring out in all the pages of the sacred Gospels. The balance is the ultimate source of affirmation for the church and the culture. In short, the model of Jesus is the scale for reform.

At the heart of any successful community, from the family to a huge corporation, is organization; excellence cannot be achieved without order and balance. The same principle applies to the parish. The distribution of power is important and complicated, with the goal that everyone participates and feels empowered. A gifted and motivated staff and membership are essential. Without a plan, chaos ensues, and communication breaks down, affecting domestic tranquility, business success, or, in the case of the parish, a vital ministry. The quickest way to destroy the well-being of a community is a lax and unsupervised staff or program.

Allowances must be made within the organization for the development of the intuitive, creative, and emotional side of life, the vantage point from which God most often speaks. The intuitive nature is the source for poetry, music, novels, and art. The dance of the Spirit meets in such places and is freed to come and go, taking us to new frontiers of the Spirit. Certainly imagination and surprising insights break out to launch and extend the implication of who we are as followers of Christ. It is within this context that I find the most encouragement and the most excitement.

Organization in the form of schedules and programs provides the framework. But we must always be mindful of our ultimate purpose. Through God's gift of *intuitive reflection*, we realize our sin and seek forgiveness and grace. It is our intuitive nature that responds to Christ's question, "What did you do for the least of mine: the lonely, the prisoner, the refugees, the poor, the children who suffer?" (Matt. 25:31–46). Reflection helps us to focus upon the reality of human nature: our pride and greed, which result in individual and collective (institutional) sin. Through intuition, we grasp the depth of mercy as it unfolds, leading us to grace and offering a more abundant life.

Communication

The message of the community begins at the door, the church narthex, where worshippers are greeted with a smile and a hand-shake. Much of the message is non-verbal, perceived as enjoyable or otherwise. The message comes from the feel and color of the place. The intuitive side of the brain is activated, collecting clues that beg the question, "Do people enjoy being here?" Nonverbal messages are transmitted in actions and reactions, revealing relationships and exposing the underlying content of the community. I am convinced that illusive, non-verbal messages are at the center, and point to the content and ultimately the strategy of what the community is about. The power of nonverbal communication is often ignored.

Communication of the message begins with the pastor, the leaders, and the willingness of the congregation to be servants. Communication is never perfect, but the intended message is love, grace, forgiveness, and solidarity with others. It is organized and gifted with as much excellence as possible, but people need to relax and realize that worship of God enables laughter, excitement, drama, and comedy. At its heart is a servant mentality. The message will never be perfect, but instead, it is marked by uniqueness and the absence of a star mentality. In Jesus mentality, integrity and acts of love and compassion are primary.

The paradigm shifts because of the simple truth that the Spirit of God does not reside in the church building but in each person. The community brings God's Spirit into the place of worship. The Spirit is within the worshippers, not the cathedral—no matter how grand it might be. God is made flesh in each renewed human being, just as God was made flesh in Jesus.

The author of John, chapter four, described Jesus' conversation with the Samaritan woman drawing water at the well. Worship at that time was centered in the temple in Jerusalem, not in the midst of everyday life. Using the metaphor of thirsting after water, Jesus revealed that he was the well that never runs dry, the pause that refreshes. He was the living water—God incarnate. Filled with this living water, the woman ran to spread the news to the community at large. As Jesus said:

> The hour is coming, and is now here, when the true worshippers will worship the Father in spirit and truth, for the Father seeks such as these to worship God in spirit and truth.
>
> —John 4:23–24

When Jesus explained to the woman that the water he had to offer "would become a spring of living water gushing up eternal life," he was reflecting upon his own baptism and belovedness and placing this beloved status on the new humanity filled with God's Spirit and living in community with God.

The sermon, the liturgy, and the music are team-focused, supported, and encouraged by a community centered upon God and his message of love. The message is biblically centered upon life, its pain and suffering, but also on its hope. Struggles are faced, and meaning is sought. Parishioners seek deeper spirituality as modeled by their pastors, who readily confess their own sins of omission and commission, acknowledging their need for grace. There are no professional shortcuts. Pastors shepherd, facilitate, invite, and encourage with Bible stories that describe the journey of faith and the path of reconciliation. Everyone is unique as part of a living body. No single person can be seen or perceived apart from his or her connection to the community. Conformity should never be the norm, but diversity should be embraced. The community is an organic whole, working, thinking, and intuiting together. All members have ownership in the congregation's life.

Leaders make mistakes, but the biggest one may come from failure to tune into the intuitive side of the brain. A balance must be sought between the cognitive, or sequence-orientated thought processes, and the emotive responses. Music, prayer, and the sacraments touch the deepest parts of our nature, where feelings and emotions rise up to move us to deeper realities.

Pastors who are not in touch with their unconscious motives may find themselves inadvertently expressing their own biases, disregarding the diversity of thought within their congregations. Consider a likeable and gifted pastor who makes a proclamation that is political and divisive. The issue is not a question of justice or injustice but one that stems from his own narrow political views, exposing deep-seated unconscious anger or unresolved resentment. Parishioners are taken aback. The pastor does not seem to realize the depth of his offense. He is a good man, but he creates an uncomfortable pain for members of his congregation because he is out of touch with his unconscious motives. Leaders and communities need to be aware of hidden, unconscious messages that reveal the conditions of their own hearts, affect communication, and send mixed messages. Listening to the unconscious and the intuitive element is important for good communication to take place.

Spirit Development

Unfortunately, the modern church's "come and see" message may be muted in redundancy or cluttered with glitter. The reality is, however, that earnest seekers come to worship because the Spirit guides them there. They are seeking God's presence. It is the work of the church to provide a living image of a world beyond what is obvious. Poets, novelists, and artists know this world. It is within their grasp.

The Spirit can commune with seekers in the intimate Chapel of the Holy Cross in Sedona, Arizona, or in the vast interior of St. Peter's Basilica in Rome. The Spirit can quietly enter a village church in the country or make an exuberant entrance into a mega church with a membership numbering in the thousands. But in each case, the worshippers are seeking an alternative environment to that which is offered in our secular world of illusions.

The name for the Spirit varies. One might call it the creative force or the energy from beyond. For some, it is the Holy Spirit or simply the Spirit. This energy, or sweetly scented spirit, moves in the midst of the people who come to see, to search for truth, and to worship the God of truth.

When pastors, leadership teams, and congregants are open to one another and to the Spirit, the atmosphere is charged with love and kindness. Trust grows in this circle of centered, thoughtful humanity. The Spirit is the leavening agent; without it, the ambiance is flat. The worship grows and the excitement builds as the people mature in their faith experiences and in their connections to one another as God's children.

The dance of the Spirit enters the music and is captured in the liturgy. It comes through the reading of Scripture and through the Word spoken from the pulpit. It comes both because of and in spite of meticulous planning. It enters on the serendipitous wings of a bird as it flies into the sanctuary. It pads in on little cat feet down the aisle in the middle of the sermon. It enters with a child's unexpected verbal contribution during the children's sermon or in a familiar voice lifted in song. It comes when a prayer request is offered and when a celebration is announced. The Spirit comes in palatable, pin-dropping silence as a beloved worshipper collapses to the floor. This same Spirit moans a prayer when words fail.

The Spirit comes in the Lord's Supper, where living words and living realities invade our illusions. Framed in reverence, the community is drawn into the experience. The bread is broken; the wine is poured. As we proceed to the table, our hearts are unexpectedly softened. We take the bread; we receive the wine. Touched by sacred mystery, we become Christ's living body, bound together by his Spirit as children of God. The experience changes us; the awe-inspiring connection humbles us. That is what Jesus meant when he asked John's disciples the rhetorical question, "What are you looking for?" Knowingly, Jesus offered, "Come and see" (John 1:38).

What people are looking for, I call the *holy places*—where everyone is intensively present in the Spirit of God. The place of mystery is touched. I call this "the place of the beloved." I sense that when we perceive the feeling of belovedness, we have touched God and he has touched us.

In *Listening to Your Life*, Frederick Buechner describes belovedness as, "… smelling oneself into the holy and the hidden parts of one's life." The ancient Celtic priests referred to "the in-between things," and the glimpse of such places is to see the mystery of the two worlds at the same time (p. 184). I am convinced that people grow, mature, and enjoy the utter profundity of the holy places. A holy place may occur on the bank of a pristine lake or high on a mountaintop. Holy places have been reported while flying at 32,000 feet in an airplane. They may intrude in a time of utter crisis or accompany a moment of profound joy. Unfortunately, these transcendent moments don't happen often enough in our worship centers.

The Spirit is always present in Jesus' new humanity; although, we may not always be willing to wait or listen for its message. Perhaps it is the receivers who are not in tune with its frequency.

As a young swimmer, I found myself in trouble. I was going down for the second time when a hand pulled me out. Was it God's hand? Was it the hand of a friend? I was uncertain. Yet, I sensed then, as I do now, that God's fingerprints were all over the event. In some form, that guiding hand has continued throughout my life, hidden but no less real, extended time after time.

This favor prompts the question, "Who am I that God should concern himself with me?" What is the source of my belovedness? Why isn't the grace and blessing extended to others? Or is it? Only mystery answers.

A parishioner who practiced the discipline of morning prayer was approached by a homeless woman requesting money for food. Though her day was tightly scheduled, the parishioner took time to share a meal with the woman, listen to her story, and offer advice on getting community services. As she drove home, she marveled that out of all of the destitute people on the street, she had selected this woman to help. Why? The answer came in an epiphany: "This one asked." So it is with God as we bring our petitions to him in faith, believing that our prayers will be heard.

Youth Ministry

Young adults and their children are looking for community because they are family-centered, perhaps more so than any other generation. They expect freshness in their surroundings and in the content of their learning experiences. These young parents seek health and simple things such as organized, clean, and attractive spaces for their children. They want a safe and stimulating place for their children to play and learn. They respond to the latest technology in the form of communication, such as imaginative websites, computer-generated presentations, and, yes, electronically-enhanced music. It is the look of the community and its willingness to convey its health and well-being that young adults find important.

Young people are looking for a community in which issues of culture and society are discussed and acted upon. National or world disasters, environmental issues (being green), unemployment, and social unrest are among their concerns. Communities that are willing to engage in dialogue and listen to divergent ideas are important to this demographic.

The young are present in a kind of life in which faith and hope live in a "tragic gap between what is, and what could and should be," according to Parker J. Palmer in "The broken-open heart: Living with faith and hope in the tragic gap," published in *Weavings* (March/April 2009). Palmer writes:

> A congregation whose members bury their difference and division for fear that surfacing them will blow the "community" apart is neither a true community nor a place where people can learn a cruciform way of life. We don't learn to love from being talked at, but from being around love in action. We don't learn to hold tension in ways that open the hearts by reading essays, but by being around others who keep learning how to do it and invite us to try it for ourselves. (p. 14)

This tragic gap between "what is and what could and should be" may have been in the mind of Henri Nouwen when, in *The Only Necessary Thing*, he explained that "we are all wounded people" (p. 150).

Meanwhile, our society rejects the premise and proposes that upward mobility is the answer to our woundedness. It is precisely here that the church community may have also missed the mark. Nouwen writes, "Those whom we love and those who love us wound us too" (p. 150). The young ones, if not all of us, feel the rejection. They have felt abused, manipulated, and deserted by those closest to them—parents, friends, spouses, school friends, teachers, and pastors. They are wounded by institutions and professions that betray their giftedness, their callings, and their life purposes.

If the church community has ignored the reality of the wounds, it may also have eliminated the source of forgiveness, the acknowledgement of sin, and the grace and power to heal. The degree to which the church community has lived the crucified way of life determines its power to bridge the gap between sin and grace (p. 123–135). Incarnation of God's Spirit in the young was demonstrated by Jesus when he drew the children around him and declared that "of such is the kingdom of God" (Mark 10:13–16). Ministering to our youth through Christian education, while engaging them in meaningful ministry, is a primary paradigm shift to be made.

The editor of *Christian Century* (Oct. 21, 2008) chastises the Christian community through the pen of influential Catholic theologian Yves Congar, who complains that the church's preachers and parish leaders too often speak like people without a spiritual life of their own, failing to live the things they preach. He complains further that they fail to address the life situations of their congregants. In other words, they fail to bridge the tragic gap between "what is and what could and should be" (p. 8).

Tom Ehrich, quoted earlier, suggests that all pastors on a specific Sunday, without any preparation on the part of the congregation, ask their congregants to name the question they would ask God and put it on an index card provided in the bulletin. These questions would be published the following Sundays in a series of sermons.

The young ones, if not all of us, expect the Christian community to address and struggle through things, even into a vale of tears if necessary, in order to address the gaps and the wounds in their lives.

Finally, the young expect sacred trust in their communities, with trust earned and lived as a transaction within the community. They expect trust to be action-orientated and valued as an interaction that endows relationships within community. The trust begins with the pastor, but if the community does not embody trust in its own life, no one sermon or person can change a hidden system of doing things.

Listening

To listen effectively is a difficult discipline. The word *listen* is rendered from the Greek *Akou'o* and means *to hear*. At Jesus' transfiguration, a voice spoke from a bright cloud, "This is my Son, the Beloved; with him I am well pleased; Listen to him!" (Matt. 17:5). *Akou'o* implies a kind of listening with all the senses. The text conveys that Jesus, recognizing his followers' fear, calmed them. He touched them and reassured them. He listened to them. (See Matt. 17:7–8).

To listen is to hear and to understand. Listening to God suggests a kind of quietness that only solitude and prayer can provide. Isaiah, a prophet and poet, described such a place as the source of strength and inner rest (Isa. 30:15). Elijah, often quoted, found God in the "still small voice" (1 Kings 19:12). Thus, to listen involves understanding and a willingness to act. The power of the encounter with God is in its clarity and intimacy.

Jesus' conversation with the Jewish rabbi Nicodemus is another good example. "You can't see the wind," Jesus said. "But you can feel it; you notice the wind's effects. You can't explain the source of the wind's power. Yet the wind is there and you can hear the wind if you listen" (John 3:1–21). St. Paul takes the conversation further when he suggests the bridge to the supernatural is to listen and to seek divine help (Rom. 8:26).

More current writers, such as Frederick Buechner and Henri Nouwen, suggest that to be an effective listener, one must be close to the culture and the world of the present. Buechner, in *Listening to Life,* writes that there is no event too commonplace that God is not present in it—if we could listen to him or allow ourselves room to recognize him (p. 51).

Buechner suggests that we have to put a frame around events to hear God's voice. A frog jumps. He lands in a pond. We observe.

The stillness is broken in the pond. Gradually the surface returns to its stillness. There is a frame around the moment if we take notice. Art conveys a message in a similar way. Rembrandt paints the parable of the Prodigal. He frames the message so the viewer may bring focus to the figures and perceive the message.

Musicians frame their messages with sound, silence, and rhythm. They express joy and praise; they touch sorrow and grief. They provide the order of time and beat for the dance, for drama, and for song, but none of it would be possible without the frame to focus our willingness to listen, observe, and feel.

Nature, with all its complexity, is framed in the rhythm of the sea as it beats upon the shore. It is captured in a mother's steady heartbeat providing life and comfort to an unborn child. The rhythm is restful when listened to and interpreted. Art, music, and nature all provide framed admonitions that say to us "Pay attention! Listen!"

Nouwen is convinced that to listen is a new way to pray, and the focus is to listen to the heart, to the sacred text, to the church, and finally, to the body. He calls the focus *disciplines*, following the tradition of the desert fathers and placing them in the context of the modern world. I sense the relevance of his work is just beginning to be perceived and grasped in the contemporary society.

Evaluation

"Metrics matter," writes Tom Ehrich (Church Wellness Report, Oct. 4, 2007). It is hard to measure without some kind of measurement device and standard. We are blind without a gauge to know where we are and where we have been.

The best means to measure group process is together and from the ground up. One can't build a community, program, or a budget without structure and guidelines. Chaos and disorder are not enablers; they destroy the best efforts.

One church has a large clock projected upon the screen to mark the countdown to the beginning of worship. But the countdown at the end is equally important! It is important to finish at the appointed time.

Programs that fail should be reviewed and filed as lessons learned. Programs that work should be evaluated, celebrated, and recorded as successes. Completed programs—whether involving music or liturgy, the projection of words on a screen, or the use of a painting or a dramatic presentation—need to be evaluated. Did people understand? Did the images catch their attention? Did people have fun? Were they able to grieve, to identify, or to feel the "buzz" of the community? Did the children enjoy worship? Did children participate at the levels of their comfort? How loose or how structured is the church? How participative are the members?

One can learn from both failure and success. But unless there is some form of evaluation, how will you know which occurred and why? How do you determine which parts are working well and which programs need adjusting? Church communities are dynamic, with ever-changing needs. Building, rebuilding, and defining communities takes time. Community trust is often fragile and requires time to develop. Sometimes, years are required to measure the outcomes, but ongoing evaluation of each process is essential.

It is normal practice to evaluate pastors and staff, but the results are too often shelved or ignored. *Best practice* requires assessing the results. Operating programs without the benefit of assessment means that energies may not be spent in the most effective manner. Boundaries and lines of responsibility need to be clearly defined, and performance must be measured and assessed. Expectations should be noted and lines of authority clearly defined.

Trust can be measured, vulnerability considered, and safeguards ensured. The key to trust is accountability and the sharing of power, as Barbara Blodgett observed in her study and recorded in *Lives Entrusted.* She wrote, "The most hopeful sign of 'trust worthiness' in a leader may be where she consistently seeks ways to empower others, thus distributing even her own power throughout the community" (p. 121). The invitation to evaluate also invites an opportunity to celebrate successes.

What does a parish look like when it employs these *best practices*? Its individual members are profoundly empowered in their personal lives, and then their families, communities, and world benefit from their individual and collective contributions. Mature Christians, living out their faith, reflect God's intention for his creation, promoting compassion and inviting reconciliation. One is drawn into this community by the Spirit; newcomers report a sense of arriving, of coming home; members express a strong sense of belonging; and pastors glow with a curious mix of humility and pride.

The exception to any measured evaluation is ultimately in God's assessment. In the end, a lifetime of service must be assessed by God himself, and I expect this is what is meant by the Final Judgment.

Chapter 2

Bridges to Spirituality

God's Spirit provides bridges to spirituality. Like the baptism of Jesus, one's baptism begins the process of life in the Spirit. The process, or paradigm shift into wholeness, is equally valid in a child or in an adult. A new pattern has begun—the integration of mind and spirit.

The bridges continue to build around the concepts of "seeing and believing" and "believing in order to see." Both perspectives are essential to spirituality. Often the desire to see or be touched by God is so strong that some folks cannot believe without their world being shaken in some way. Such was the case with St. Thomas.

The story of the disciple Thomas's reluctance to believe in Jesus' resurrection and his need to touch Christ's nail-scarred hands is recorded in John 20:24–29. Thomas was stuck in unbelief. He was caught in his present reality.

In contrast, when the journey to spirituality begins with belief, the embodiment of the Spirit of Jesus enables sight. The first perspective is focused on the present knowledge, while the second looks toward a future reality. Both involve incarnation, and both enable one's spirituality to be grounded in historical reality (Waetjen, p. 139). One cannot expect either perspective to have greater validity. However, "to believe in order to see" may well enable the intuitive mind to become more operative as one looks to the future. Dreams, visions, synchronicity, and other manifestations of right-brain activity may be the source for building faith and seeing ultimate reality or divining truth. The incarnation of God's Spirit is the key to this paradigm shift in the individual and in the community of faith.

How do we build mystical bridges between our spiritual and sensory perceptions? How do we find a pathway between the temporal and eternal, between the conscious and the unconscious? One answer is found in Matthew's and Mark's accounts of the imprisonment of John the Baptist. John sends his disciples to find Jesus. He needs to be reassured that Jesus is indeed the Messiah. He needs to answer the question, "Is Jesus the bridge between man and God?" Jesus gives a pragmatic answer, an invitation to come and see what has occurred: "The blind find sight, the dead find life, and the poor have good news brought to them." Jesus assures John, "Don't be offended, know you are blessed without equal; you have prepared bridges to the Almighty, you have prepared the Way" (Matt. 11:2–19 and Luke 7:18–35).

Jesus bemoans the woes of his generation—chastising those unable to hear, those who refuse to listen, ignoring the bridge made for them (Matt. 11:16–24). Jesus explains that children understand these spiritual principals intuitively. Totally dependent on their earthly caretakers, they approach life in a spirit of trust and carefree abandon. Then life happens. A hurt here, a disappointment there, a handful of broken promises, and resentment grows. Earthly wisdom and education confound our once childlike faith.

Translated into terms of the modern culture, the bridge to the mystical is intuitive. To one who is weary and one who suffers or is burdened, the reconnection of the Spirit is profound. In suffering, we recognize our need for healing. We seek the solace of a gentle and humble heart, yearning for a spiritual rest—a place of simplicity and clarity amidst the cacophony of our complex culture (Matt. 11:25–30). The answer is clear: Jesus is that bridge to the "hidden mysteries" of life. No rocket science or intellectual reasoning is required. In our prayers, we are told to approach God as a child might approach a loving parent. Like the repentant thief on the cross, who asked only to be remembered in Jesus' kingdom, the simplest request crosses the bridge to the world beyond our senses. In Matthew 11:28 Christ invites, "Come to me, all who labor and are heavy laden and I will give you rest. Take my yoke upon you and learn of me. For I am gentle and lowly in heart, and you will find rest for your soul, for my yoke is easy and my burden is light."

The Celtic Way

In this vortex between two worlds, the church has struggled with varying levels of success, attempting to understand these hidden mysteries. The search for the hidden mysteries has been a journey for many to rediscover their faith. For some, the answers have been found in the roots of Celtic spirituality and the holy ground of Celtic Christianity. Ivan Bradley, in his book *The Celtic Way*, describes the pathos of lost paths to the sacred. The parish, from his perception, has been polarized between a kind of emotional sentimentality and intellectual selectivity. The result has left the parish barren and without meaning. Bradley writes:

> Two powerful contradictory trends threaten the integrity and perhaps even the survival of contemporary western Christianity.

One would turn it into a highly abstract and conceptualized academic discipline appealing only to intellectuals while the other would reduce it to a series of shallow emotional slogans. In both cases, what is at risk is an understanding of the element of mystery, which is at the heart of the Christian faith. (p. 84)

Bradley suggests that the bridge to the Celtic mystery is the power of imagination expressed in the Celts' faith symbols. The Celtic ability to capture images and express in poetry their visions, dreams, and premonitions was readily adapted to everyday living. Celtic icons, standing crosses, and stones were powerful images that provided tangible bridges to their spirituality. The Celts were open to God's presence because their symbols were intertwined with their daily work and play. Creation was alive with the presence of God and always close to them. Imagination held the key to the broad appreciation of the sacred and holy places of worship (p. 93). Everything was seen as good in nature and to be enjoyed. God was close to them and involved in every personal part of their living. They naturally gave thanks to him.

The Celts were a people who enjoyed dialogue, meditation, and the touch of God's voice in nature. They shared their lives and discovered themselves in community. They opposed religious domination or the use of force to bring about an uncomfortable conversion. Their ability to close the gap between various cultural differences by adapting them into the Christian faith was noteworthy. The standing stones, the sacred graves, the shrines of healing, the power of circles, and their deep interest in the in-between things were acknowledged by the early missionaries and incorporated into Christian worship and the preaching of the gospel (p. 94). Bradley suggests that such an outlook lends itself to the modern mind and heart. Man's hunger for the sacred mysteries, common to the early Celts, is equally felt in the modern community.

Contemporary man or woman seeks to satisfy the hunger for the in-between things described by the early Celtic mystics or Druids as they observed nature. One of nature's examples is mistletoe, which is neither a plant nor a tree. Mist is not quite rain and not quite air. A dream is neither waking nor sleeping. These in-between places invite the soul to search, to make use of imagination, to follow creative hunches, and to zigzag in his or her thinking.

These in-between places can also be found in works of art, music, or poetry, in which the sense of sight and sound vacillate between realities and perceptions. Vincent Van Gogh's *Field of Poppies* first appears as a plowed field, but on a more careful examination, the red paint strokes sprout poppies! The power and beauty of the artist's genius becomes clear. The work's appeal crosses the bridge to the sacred and to beauty itself.

Esther DeWaal in *The Celtic Way of Prayer* directs the imagination in her search for spirituality. She immerses herself in Celtic prayers and rides the imagination to sacred places. She defines imagination, quoting Thomas Merton, as the essential element in prayer and spirituality:

> Imagination is the creative task of making symbols, joining things together in such a way that they throw new light on each other and on everything around them. The imagination is a discovering faculty; a faculty for seeing relationships, for seeing meaning that is special and even quite new. The imagination is something which enables us to discover unique present meaning in a given

moment of our life. Without imagination, the contemplative life can be extremely dull and fruitless. (p. xiv)

DeWaal suggests that most people are battered by a succession of superficial images that are filled with meaningless, static, or mindless chatter. Therefore, the recovery of fundamental images

that engage one's imagination is essential. Fire, wind, bread, water, light and dark, and heart and passion are meaningful images that are worthy to engage spirituality (p. 36–37).

Brain Studies

It is not my intent to provide a historical study of the function of the brain, nor to oversimplify the complexities, but rather to report upon recent findings and a unique journey of one brain scientist who suffered a stroke and recorded her findings as she recovered. The implications may well open the door to understanding the pathway to spirituality. She is Dr. Jill Bolte Taylor, a neuroanatomist, who, at the time of her stroke, was a research and teaching scholar at Harvard Medical School, specializing in neuroanatomy in the department of neuroscience.

On December 10, 1996, she awoke to discover she had a brain disorder of her own. She suffered a massive stroke to the left part of her brain. Her experience and insights gained are not just rare, they are also unique. They may confirm what has been suspected but never acknowledged between the disciplines of religion and science: that our mutual understanding of human spirit and body are closer than we realize.

Until recently, medical science has been closely focused upon what can be perceived through the senses, the organism, and the physical. It has ignored the mystical and tolerated the emotional and psychological as soft science. Taylor's ability to understand the insights gained is also noteworthy. Her analysis of human energy or life force breaks new ground—revealing truth readily available but not yet understood.

She found as she began her early recovery that she could not use language or understand it. Yet she was acutely aware of people's energy. She became empathic to what others felt. Body language, facial expressions, and energy dynamics were keys to her experience. She described people as concentrated packages of energy, either as sources for healing or causes for alarm (p. 74–75). In one case, the unwillingness of a nurse to connect with her frightened Taylor;

she did not feel safe in the nurse's care. She found it hard to cope with people exhibiting high levels of anxious energy, while those evoking love and kindness had a way of healing. Nervous, anxious, or angry people were counterproductive to her recovery. She called them "energy vampires" (p. 75).

Taylor's purpose in writing of her recovery is best put in her own words: "Ultimately, my book is about my brain's journey into my right hemisphere's consciousness, where I became enveloped in deep inner peace. I have resurrected the consciousness of my left hemisphere in order to help others achieve that same inner peace, without having to experience stroke" (p. 3).

Taylor's journey to recovery is intriguing. She describes firsthand the right side of the brain. The right brain processes information in pictures; it is the source of spontaneous emotions; it is caring and imaginative; it demonstrates the ability to be empathic; it is the source for intuition and "hunch" kind of creativity; it thinks out of the box. It sees the big picture; its orientation is in the now (p. 30).

The left brain processes information in a completely different way. It is detailed and focused; it organizes in lineal and methodical forms. It is conscious of time—past, present, and future (p. 31); it is obsessed with words. Words are key elements to describe, define, categorize, and communicate. Additionally, the left brain is excited with details and facts; it excels in academics and dominates the whole brain with its importance and skill. It speaks almost constantly with what is called "brain chatter," often to the point of exasperation. The left hemisphere creates what Taylor calls "loop of thought patterns" (p. 32). More importantly, the left hemisphere demonstrates an aptitude and ability to be critical and judgmental and to analyze. It may be the source of integrity, honesty, and generosity. It also may be the center of independence and survival. The left hemisphere is unique and may be the source of the ego.

Each hemisphere, however, compliments the other. They work intimately together. The left side is language orientated. The right centers on non-verbal communication. Body language and detection of hidden messages are not picked up by the left hemisphere. The left hemisphere interprets everything literally, so it is in need of the input that touches emotion and evaluates deeper intent, humor, light-hearted communications, or anger and threats from the right (p. 33).

Overall, Taylor's observation is that our western society honors the left hemisphere more than the right hemisphere. Western society, unfortunately for imagination, poetry, and music, often gets lost in the dominate domain of the left hemisphere. In Taylor's opinion, there is a deep need to rediscover the power of the right hemisphere and its productive avenue to spirituality and creativity. The right hemisphere may be what helps fuel grace, love, compassion, and forgiveness.

To Taylor, the right side is the source for adventure, adaptation, and connection to others. It is the seat of the "divine mind." It is the knower, the wise woman, and the observer of the sacred. In the right hemisphere, intuition and higher consciousness is clearly observed (p. 140). Taylor's chief contribution may be to remind us all that we are "energy beings" and that we have the need to become aware of our own energy dynamics and intuitions (p. 167).

Taylor observes what everyone knows, but few consider valid: that instinct and intuition can be relied upon. For example, we like certain people because there is energy between us and them. We just like them. They twinkle with something. They encourage response, while others pull back, withdraw, or disengage. Taylor's insight is a part of the energy dynamics discovered in her eight years of recovery. It touches upon mystery, both in the medical and the religious world. Her words are more than adequate for both disciplines. She writes:

> On an energy level, if I think about you, send good vibrations your way, hold you in the light, or pray for you, then I am consciously sending my energy to you with healing intention. If I meditate over you, or lay my hands upon your wound, then I am purposely directing energy of my being to help you heal. (p. 168)

A second generation of neuroscientists, called synthesizers, have built upon the raw data of the first brain scientists and provided integration of views on the brain, mind, and the body as it works in relationships. David Siegel and his associate, Bonnie Badenoch, the author of *Being a Brain-Wise Therapist,* are synthesizers. The former, the guide and teacher, and the latter, a therapist working with those in suffering, both focus on the processes and energy of the brain, mind, and body as they integrate together. For the therapist, the focus has been upon the right hemisphere and its integration into the whole brain and the healing of suffering experiences. Her work as a therapist has provided deep insights into the empathic relationship of the therapist and the sufferer. Her focus began in the exploration of the best way to enter a person's world of suffering by first understanding how the brain works, then establishing and maintaining right-brain-to-right-brain connections. The process of listening empathetically, understanding the mind, being comfortable with insights about the way the brain works, experiencing the history of the sufferer, and supporting the patient's ability to help bring healing of emotional wounds and distorted relationships are the elements for helping the sufferer according to Siegel and Badenoch (p. xi–xiii).

Badenoch's findings on brain function are similar to Taylor's analysis but differ in focus. Badenoch's is more theory to practice. She has found that the two hemispheres are similar in structure to Taylor's but process information and experiences differently. She defines the two types of processing as left-mode processing (LMP) and right-mode processing (RMP). The left hemisphere (LMP) enjoys logic, linearity, language, and literalness. It enjoys sequence: A, and then B, then C is a staircase kind of processing. It loves words. It explains feelings, but it does not understand feelings or experience feeling. The process of the left brain is predictable in terms of cause-and-effect patterns. Left hemisphere (LMP) is wired by order. It functions on a yes/no, right/wrong binary system (p. 19).

However, Badenoch's greater interest is in the function and processes of the right hemisphere. The right-mode processes are more whole in perception and non-linear. This side of the brain processes the visual and spatial inputs. It receives the non-verbal signals in social contexts and interprets and sends its input to the left brain. Such concerns as self-image, the world, and relationships are felt and processed. It is concerned with perception of the events of the day, personal history, and the journey of the person. It is out of the right hemisphere (RMP) that we process understanding of self and others. The right hemisphere seems to be the center of emotions such as love, pain, and spirituality. Badenoch suggest there is a language in the right hemisphere. It is ambiguous/emotion and image laden and a kind of poetry (p. 19–20). It processes a special *knowing*. It may be a language of dreams, visions, intuitions, and insights, even creativity. Although Badenoch is unclear as to the language, she argues that the right hemisphere is the center and the bedrock for healing (p. 20). It provides the integration and correction enabled by the therapist's right mode of process as they connect with the patients. Inasmuch as possible, the process is a brain-to-brain, creative dance that fosters wholeness and integration of the whole body, brain, and mind (p. 21).

What is unusual and exceptional about Badenoch's experiences are her observations of the mystical. Such subjects as beliefs, religious practices, ethical behavior, and moral concerns are readily faced and brought into therapy, not avoided or fostered. Nonetheless, they are handled with care and awareness of their intangibility. She cautions against projection of any negative views that may lay hidden in the therapist and the potential misery that may occur through distorted understanding, an inability to understand the suffering within the patient or his or her mutual struggles to understand the mystical. The work of the therapist is to promote emotional clarity and to create a healing atmosphere (p. 96).

From such an open stance toward spirituality—neither avoidance nor fostering—the manifestation of a deeper sense of hope, compassion, and goodness is possible. It might be what Siegel would whisper, but not too loudly, as "transpiration integration" or the integrated brain (p. 96). It is no small wonder that a neuroscientist and a brain-wise therapist have, however tentatively, crossed the street to explore spirituality as a potential source of healing in the modern world.

Chapter 3

Paradigm of the Parish

The Energy

To understand paradigm shifts is to understand the incarnation of God in the man—Jesus. The implication is to become a part of Jesus' new humanity, empowered by God's Spirit. "Old things have passed away and all things have become new," writes St. Paul (2 Cor. 5:17). God dwells within a person to do God's ministry. As sons and daughters of God in a modern culture, and as the living, incarnate people of God, the new human beings become the source of paradigm shifts within the culture. We provide the pattern and the doorways to God. The pattern is empowered by God's living Spirit. Thus, the spoken Word is empowered by God's living Spirit to do his work in the new human beings. The indwelling Spirit inspires, creates, and heals through the new man or new woman.

The word *paradigm* is defined as fixed forms contained in a particular element. The form may have a single root, stem, or theme. For example: *boy, boys, and boy's* constitute the paradigm of the noun *boy.* From the Greek word *paradigm,* the meaning is defined as a "pattern."

In terms of the paradigm of the parish, the form is more organic and interconnected. The spirit of a community is linked to the primary identity as energy. In this respect, the energy of each person is linked to that of the whole community. The New Testament calls this energy the *paraclete,* defined in the *Interpreter's Dictionary of the Bible* as "one called alongside," both in a passive form as one who stands with or alongside and one who is active as an advocate or counselor, who gives strength and comfort (p. 654).

Two passages in St. John's gospel refer to the *paraclete,* illustrating both the passivity and activity of the Spirit. St. John's treatment represents the most highly developed thoughts on the personality of the Spirit in the New Testament, according to the *Interpreter's Dictionary of the Bible.* The first passage promises that the Advocate as a helper will "be with the disciples forever" (John 14:16). The Advocate will teach and remind them of all that Jesus has said. The Advocate will become an indwelling, personal presence at home with them (John 14:26).

The second example is more poetic; nonetheless, it is profoundly descriptive of the divine energy of the Holy Spirit. The passage is called "the true-vine-stock" teaching. God, the Father, tends the branches grafted into the divine stock. The indwelling energy is the source and the dynamic within the vine. The results are "objective fruit bearing" (John 15:1–9). The indwelling creates God's work and the potential to exceed Jesus' work (John 14:12).

The third *paracletic* passage comes from St. Paul. He too draws on an organic image. He explicitly calls the community "the body of Christ." The body is the living, energized community. The individual person, just like the branches on the vine, is connected to the body. Therefore, the body becomes the paradigm of the community (1 Cor. 12:11–12).

Henri Nouwen, in *The Only Necessary Thing*, reflects on St. Paul's words as revealing "the energy" as part of prayer within the person. Prayer then becomes the bridge between the inner parts of the individual. He writes, "Prayer is the bridge between my unconscious and conscious life. Prayer connects my mind with my heart, my will with my passions, and my brain with my belly. Prayer is the way to let the life-giving spirit of God penetrate all the corners of my being. Prayer is the divine instrument of my wholeness, unity, and inner peace" (p. 35–36).

Nouwen invites us to live in the midst of the world without being caught in the nets of wounds and needs. Prayer provides the interruption. "The energy of God" breaks the interlocking dependencies that are often a part of daily life. What he suggests requires a rethinking of the concept of God, his community, and the spirituality of the person. He suggests a new way of being together, of being in community. The links become more authentically tied to the person, the community, and their spirituality. He suggests a new way "to know" who one is and where one belongs. Nouwen's thoughts are radical in their simplicity, yet profoundly complex. He suggests a way to grasp mystery based upon St. Paul's teachings (p. 25).

Another look at the *paracletics* is found in St. Luke's gospel (Luke 10:38–42). Jesus enters a village where a woman named Martha welcomes him into her home. Her sister, Mary, sits at Jesus' feet, listening to him. Meanwhile, Martha becomes distracted by the task of hospitality. She protests to Jesus about Mary's inactivity. Jesus' response has left a legacy of dynamic tension in the church ever since. The story illustrates the dichotomy between the business of the church and the work of the Spirit. Jesus reminds Martha of the importance of listening, of being present and available to the Spirit. The meaning of the episode, as Fitzmyer notes in *The Anchor Bible*, is not a condemnation against the active life or against the hospitality of Martha, but it is one that expects the contemplative to be joined to a life of action (p. 892). Thus the energy or spirit finds its source of renewal in contemplation and a source of "knowing" who one is and what one is to do as one grasps mystery in the world of culture.

If one is to speak to or propose a new paradigm for the parish, one must do so with a balance of the active and the meditative mind. In Jesus' estimation, "Mary has chosen the better part" (Luke 10:42). Thus, to be a paradigm that begins in the contemplative is not only explicit and radical, but also it is as fragmentary as a dream and as undefined as intuition. Nonetheless, the paradigm provides a rediscovered way of thinking, a pathway to listening, and a means of rediscovering God and his spiritual energy.

Frederick Buechner, in his book *Listening to Your Life*, captures this tension when he suggests a different kind of person to whom one's ideas and one's experiences are inseparable. That is to say, one cannot speak or write about God or sin or grace apart from speaking or writing about one's own experiences. One's ideas become compelling and real because they have been experienced (p. 80).

A boy often sits with other boys of the same age in an open-air theater at a church camp located high in the mountains. A blind man plays his music, and the boy is touched by mystery. This solitary man, unsighted in the traditional sense, translates his insight, his vision to the heart of the boy. Compelling and real, the musical message moves the boy. Several years later, in a country church, a storyteller's words touch the boy again. This time, the energy is more direct, yet equally valid. The idea to be a pastor, poet, or a priest is planted. Gradually, the initial experience, real and compelling, bathed in mystery, gains focus. These were my experiences that propelled me on my faith journey, that led to a degree, ordination, pastoral ministry, and finally, to the writing of this book.

Lutheran Theologian Joseph Settler, from the University of Chicago, observes in *Gravity and Grace* that there are realities to which terms point, while escaping specifications. No words are sufficient or adequate to precisely define these realities. They elude the scope of a fine-point pen; they can only be described as realities. Imagination, energy (spirit), and prayer are three examples of realities with undefined specifications (p. 25).

With this in mind, the one step toward renewed sources of energy in the parish may lie in the ability of the parish to recognize and embrace its tenuous life caught in the tension between Christ's teachings and the culture of its time. Anthony Bloom, in *Beginning to Pray*, suggests that Christians live in three worlds, while our society and culture live in only two. He would argue that too much of our theological training has been focused on culture and society and too little on the spiritual or eternal realm (p. 18). The parish, like its society, has lived in the world of darkness and light and has been uncomfortable with the tension. In some ways, the parish has retreated from the darkness to the point of being incompatible with and irrelevant to modern life. The tragedy of 9-11 and the ongoing War on Terror has awakened us, causing many to reexamine the reality of darkness with all its insidious complexity.

Esther DeWaal, in *Every Earthly Blessing*, holds that the third dimension, that of the Spirit, may be approached in the Celtic way. Spirit cannot be understood in cerebral terms. It speaks to the heart. Like poetry, it defies definition and remains ultimately illusive (p. 9). The Celtic tradition harnesses the energy of the Spirit through prayer, meditation, and imagination. Celtic practices provide a viable model for the parish and its parishioners.

Bloom's thoughts on the third world and the Celtic way of perception with its use of imagination and symbols may well lead to the path of rediscovery. The following is a prayer I wrote in meditation. It describes the world of imagination and uses poetry to describe the focus of the heart and the world of eternity through which the mystical energy may heal the person and provide understanding.

Our Friend in the Shadows

Good Friend
Whose words come so frequently.
Come to us
When we feel
Helpless
And weak.
Good friend
Move us with your compassion
Within the circle
Of old and new.
Good friend
Whose love is disguised
Touch those closest to us.
Let not our litany of repetition
Weary You
Nor keep you from hearing
Our plea.
Good Friend
Shepherd of these personal and quiet
Moments where striking and
Chiming clocks mark the
Passing thoughts and words.
Draw our worlds together
So that the "sparkling images"
Of Your world may touch ours.
Good Friend
In the shadows
Heal the deep wounds
Created by misplaced acts
Faulted perceptions
And touch the sensitive parts
No one else knows.

—**Chet B. Gean**
from *Thoughts in Time* ©2003

The Celtic way is to listen to the world from the personal experience of nature, of symbols, and of the ongoing struggle between good and evil. These experiences become validated life energy that resonates within the person. With imagination and intuition, energy is received from experience; the energy becomes kinetic, and the right hemisphere connects, unless it is blocked by conditioning or hindered by lack of use.

As I mentioned before, Jill Bolte Taylor, in her experiential and personal brain study, suggests that we are "energy beings." The right hemisphere is designed to perceive and decipher the subtle energy of another person, group, or workplace. We perceive the energy intuitively, if the right hemisphere is allowed to do its work. As energy beings, we are designed to perceive and translate the kinds of energy we experience. To the medical world, the right hemisphere is a mystery. The medical culture is strongly dominated by left-brain-oriented people. If they cannot smell it, taste it, hear it, see it, or touch it, they tend to be skeptical of its existence (p. 167).

The Written Word

The plight of the parish, as I have noted, is that the parish is so dominated by the "cultural" that it ignores the kinetic sources of energy, imagination, spirituality, dreams, intuition, and the potential healing by God's Spirit. Buechner, in *Secrets in the Dark*, describes "kinetic experience" as the avenue or conduit through which the writer opens his veins from his experience of reality to the reader. It is autobiographical. Words go from the writer directly into the bloodstream of the reader at full strength! If there is poison in the writer's words, the reader is poisoned. If the words give nourishment, the reader is nourished. Buechner's concept comes from the Hebrew word *dabbar*. It means that word and deed are interconnected. Word and experience go together. *Dabbar*, he suggests, is creative energy, or to put it in the terms of the parish, *the living presence of God*, fashioned out of the raw events of the parish experience. He notes the same elusive and ambiguous characterization of the poet. Nonetheless, as a writer, he is surprised too often by intuition and imagination as he shapes his novels. He confesses that the energy becomes the arms and the legs to creativity and inner strength; this energy opens doors to all of us. Buechner writes:

> As a writer, I strive to proclaim as convincingly and as honestly as I can, the most interesting observations I have made in the world as I have experienced it. At the top of my list is my discovery of the elusive presence of God in our midst. I try not to stack the deck or load the dice in my favor, but rather to be as true to my experience of the dark and despairing side as to the holy and hopeful side. The "elusive presence" is my continuous subject, and one that often raises eyebrows and sparks suspicion. Those exceptional writers who dare to examine their lives candidly, searchingly and with feeling and report back their findings to the rest of us are noteworthy. (p. 123–130)

We need the eyes of writers like Buechner to gain insight. May their courageous blood course through our veins!

The Psalms and Old Testament prophets frequently speak to contemplative minds. Their prayers, worship, and meditations have often found expression in poetry. The greatest intuitive source in the New Testament, in many minds, is St. John's gospel. If there is a mystic in the New Testament, John is one. His work has been called the "Pearl of Great Price" by some scholars, according to Raymond E. Brown in *S.S.: Anchor Bible, Vol. 19*. If that is true, then John's prologue is a pearl within a pearl (p. 18), one of the finest poetic descriptions to engage the mind and the heart of the reader.

Poets and poetry are not in vogue in most intellectual circles. Poets have lost their place and been marginalized in parish life as well. Prose is seen as more direct and precise. It has drama and intrigue and leads the mind as a story unfolding its content. It appeals to the left hemisphere of the brain. Poetry, on the other hand, touches the heart issues. It taps into the great strength of the right hemisphere of the mind, almost as a painting captures the eye in color and message. Herman C. Waetjen in his book, *The*

Gospel of the Beloved Disciple, holds that nowhere in the Bible is the power of poetry more evident than in the prologue to St. John's gospel. John's prologue does what all good poetry does: it engages the world of the mystic and touches eternity. John's perspective is a Hellenistic Jewish Christian's understanding of God in creation and of God's communication in sacred history and in the revelation, "… thus said the Lord" (p. 63).

John's prologue is called "The Logos Poem or Hymn." Raymond Brown, in *The Anchor Bible, The Gospel According to John*, explains that the lines in the poem exhibit a form sequence or staircase parallelism, whereby one word is prominent in one line, often the predicable or last word, and repeated in the next verse (p. 19). Waetjen, in *The Gospel of the Beloved Disciple*, goes on to say that the central figure of the poems is Logos, the Word; however, it is a different kind of word. It is a proper name, but more than that, the Logos or Word is a form of energy. It is the agent of creation, not only in terms of the cosmos but also as the agent of mystical energy and insight. It is wondrous and the figure of movement in sacred history, co-existing with God as the "consummate figure" to bring light into darkness (p. 73–80). The Logos is the "consummate human being" and the prototype of humanity. The Logos is the creative Word. He is Jesus, the Word that calls forth Lazarus from the dead. He is the Word that is life, gives life, and stirs up life. The Logos, the Word, has the touch of God in him, just as our words have our touch within them.

In short, the Logos is the generating holy energy that is expressed in creation, in language, and in physical touch. The Logos is the intuitive Light to guide the heart and mind of new human beings. The Logos represents the paradigm shift in the perception of God into human form. He is the Living Word or sacred Logos.

Herman Waetjen captures the concept of Logos in the darkness in his analysis of John 1:1–5:

> There is "the darkness" that is also present and active in context
> of the historical activity of the Logos. It is not the darkness of
> the creative act of the Logos; it is the darkness resulting from

the *Fall*, and therefore, the darkness that is the fundamental condition of human existence in society. In verse 5a (the light shines on in the darkness) it appears to be a state or condition, in 5b, a power (for the darkness did not overcome it). Both, of course, oppose the light that the Logos generates. If that light is identified with truth—that keenness of mental intuition and clarity of understanding that human beings acquire through the Logos to interpret the world, "the darkness" must symbolize all the manipulation of language in society that suppresses the truth and distorts reality and fosters false consciousness. (p. 70–71)

John has described the process of the mind as it perceives the mystic world of the Logos and articulates in poetic form the "consummate figure" of the Logos, Jesus Christ. The Logos is the figure of the *new* humanity and provides the means of becoming one with oneself and God (p. 70–71). Jesus prayed that his disciples "may be one, even as you, Father are one *in* me and I *in* you, so that they may also be *in* us … I am *in* them and you *in* me, so they may be brought into completion into one" (John 17:20–23, emphasis added).

What the poet John suggests is that the Logos, the Word, is a source of energy perceived intuitively and dynamically to the point that energy is exchanged with one's human deeds. He suggests the Logos manifests the creative speech in human form of a new humanity, such that words are deeds and deeds are words interacting dynamically and kinetically in form and substance.

St. John captures this phenomenon in the story of the disciple Philip finding Nathaniel at Bethesda. Philip speaks of the Logos figure, Jesus. Nathaniel is studying under a fig tree, as was the custom of rabbis. Nathaniel asks, "Can anything good come from Nazareth?"

Philip encourages him to "come and see."

When Jesus sees Nathaniel coming toward him, he says, "Here is a true Israelite in whom there is no deceit" (John 1:43–51). Jesus identifies Nathanial as one without guile or treachery. How did Jesus know? The answer suggested by St. John is that Jesus knew Nathanial intuitively, almost as if they had met before. His mind detected an openness of spirit. The perception was non-verbal, a form of knowing or insight. John is a poet at his best, grasping and defining reality at a profound level.

The paradigm shift for the parish is to grasp the importance of God's incarnation in our thinking, our meditation, and our indwelling. Culture and evil in culture may be our most difficult barriers to overcome. In the following chapters, I will focus attention on evil and on culture as barriers to worship; on imagination as the vehicle for the paradigm shift; and on the incarnation as God's holy energy, achieving his work in new and relevant patterns of ministry.

Part 2
Evil Masked— Psychological Perspective

Chapter 4

Evil as Energy

The Myth of the Flesh

Death is an illusion
Created by the same magician
Who gave us the illusion of life.
Pain is an illusion
Created to make us believe
In the greatest illusion of all
Ourselves
And who created all these illusions
But the master of it all?

And who is he
But an illusion too
Created to keep me from you.
And who created him
But the evil one
Who is no illusion at all.
And who is he
If he exists
He is simply selfishness.
Then who is Jesus? you ask
The one who wore no mask.

—Greg Richardson
from *The Thirteenth Hour* ©2011

The most dynamic paradigm shift for our modern society may lie in our willingness to face and identify *evil* as energy that is intent on destroying the good in our culture and in the perception of the sacred. Modern theology tends to ignore the subject of evil and to trivialize the cosmic struggle. The drama of Jesus' trial, persecution, and crucifixion is an incomplete story without the struggle between good and evil. The larger cosmic drama was present at the crucifixion as darkness fell over the earth. The sun was eclipsed, and the curtain in the temple, representing the place of the holy, was ripped into two pieces. Both events represented the paradigm shift brought about by Jesus' victory over his opponent, death and darkness. God's Spirit, once confined in the temple at Jerusalem, could no longer be confined. The new humanity filled by the spirit of Jesus was incarnated by Jesus' atonement. The illusion of separation was shattered; yet the struggle continues to this day. Jesus knew it would when he prayed for his disciples and the unification of his body—the church (John 17). The paradigm shift continues into the present.

What is evil? Is the subject of evil now relegated to the domain of Hollywood—suitable only to the modern mind as entertainment, dominating our home box office viewing and producing blockbuster films? Is evil the product of illusion and superstition, or is it in fact a form of illness? Is evil to be addressed only by those on the fringe of the religious mainstream, or is it a reality that should concern us all?

Those who survived the holocaust of World War II know firsthand the insidious, destructive nature of evil. Martin Luther King, Jr., raised his voice against evil, which he witnessed as overt racism on city busses, in restaurants, and at drinking fountains. He inspired others to dismantle the covert, systemic racism in the workplace and in government. On the morning of September 11, 2001, evil's assault left its imprint on our physical and emotional landscape. We all abhor the evil propagated by child abusers and molesters. What of the evil spread by unscrupulous financiers that destroyed peace of mind and financial security for millions of Americans, or what of corporate greed, the evil that feeds our gluttonous appetites for consumption of the earth's resources? In the last century, millions have been murdered by genocidal regimes. Man's inhumanity to man continues in new venues. Today we rely on the media to make sense of the clashing swords in the Middle East and around the world, and yet media spokesmen and political figures frequently inspire horror and fear, voicing more questions than answers.

I think the greatest evil perpetrated within our borders was slavery, followed by the aftermath of the Civil War with the rise of the KKK, lynching, and the systematic dehumanization of African Americans in the South. I have a terrible feeling that the evil of racism continues to lurk just beneath the surface in many people and institutions.

What does evil mean for the modern man—secular or religious? I have wrestled evil personally as a religious leader, as a parish minister, and as a church consultant. My experiences have challenged me to revisit and to rethink the psychology of evil and, in particular, its effects upon Christianity.

In 1955, Andrew Delbanco, Professor of Humanities at Columbia University, wrote *The Death of Satan*, advancing the idea that Americans had lost their sense of evil. Could Delbanco's pronouncement accurately represent the understanding of theological institutions and parishes just ten years after the Holocaust? Is his thesis a form of repression, of denial—the sort of which we witness today? Is the devil an anachronism—a product of collective, short-term memory loss? Has there been a shift in understanding the source of evil, thus making necessary a new definition? Is our ignorance the devil's stealth weapon?

Perhaps the most poignant New Testament description of evil comes from St. John's narrative of Judas's betrayal of Jesus. The text reads, "After he [Judas] received the bread [the symbol of communion], Satan entered into him" (John 13:27). Judas's rejection and betrayal initiated a chain of events, which led to the death of Jesus and sentenced Judas to damnation.

Herman C. Waetjen, in *The Gospel of the Beloved Disciple*, described the classic, biblical struggle between good and evil and between mankind and his dark shadows. Waetjen wrote:

> Only one of the disciples is lost, destroyed by his own rejection and betrayal of Jesus. Judas is not named, but referred to as "the son of destruction," an appellative that stands in opposition to the titles that Jesus bears in the gospel, "The Son of the human being and the Son of God." Judas is therefore characterized as an opponent of God's work who has destined himself to damnation. By chewing Jesus' flesh and drinking his blood, he has participated in the divine life of the new human being. But his betrayal has negated his participation in it. Instead of crossing over from death into life by entering into *new humanity*, Jesus is pioneering; he [Judas] has become the devil. (p. 373, emphasis added)

The word *evil* in Hebrew and Greek usage denotes a pragmatic and a qualitative sense. Evil has been described as "worthless, corrupt, painful and injurious; evil means trouble, distress or calamity," particularly for mankind and uniquely in terms of Israel. Evil is a source of suffering that is endured, often in the Old Testament and predominately in the New Testament. Evil implies the wrong that mankind does and the maliciousness and perversity of the human heart (*Interpreter's Dictionary*, 1962, p. 182).

There is value in the study of evil, as Paul Kahn explained in his book *Out of Eden*. His exploration of the genealogy of evil begins first with evil as the central category within Christianity; secondly, as the characteristic of evil in Judeo-Christian tradition; and finally, as evil's emergence from religious tradition into the secular world. His work is brilliantly focused upon the roots of evil and of its opposite—good (p. 3).

I approach the subject of *evil* from both a theological and psychological perspective, and for this reason, I am drawn to the work of Reinhold Niebuhr. One classic section of his work, *Children of Light and the Children of Darkness*, deals with evil and the systems of evil present during World War II. His is a significant context from which to identify and describe evil. Niebuhr wrote:

> . . . the moral cynics who know no law beyond their will and interest (are termed) *children of darkness*. Those who believe that self-interest should be brought under the discipline of a higher law could then be termed *children of light*. This is no arbitrary device, for evil is always the assertion of a self-interest without regard to the whole, whether the whole be conceived as the immediate community, or the total community of mankind, or the total order of the world. The good, is on the other hand, always the harmony of the whole on various levels. Devotion to a subordinate and premature *whole*, such as the nation, may of course become evil, viewed from the perspective of the larger whole, such as the community of mankind. *The children of light* may thus be defined, as those who seek to bring self-interest under the discipline of a more universal law, and in harmony with a more universal good. (p. 9–10)

Eight years later, in *The Irony of American History*, Niebuhr expressed his insights succinctly and poetically:

> Nothing worth doing can be achieved in our time.
> Therefore we must be saved by hope.
> Nothing which is true or beautiful or good makes complete sense
> In any immediate context of history;
> Therefore we must be saved by faith.
> Nothing we do, however virtuous, can be accomplished alone;
> Therefore we are saved by love.

No virtuous act is quite as virtuous from the standpoint of friend
    or foe
As it is from our stand point;
Therefore we must be saved by the final form of love,
Which is forgiveness.

—The Progressive Christian,
November–December, 2008

It is particularly noteworthy that Niebuhr approaches evil and goodness as perhaps no other writer does: in the context of a world war, in terms of nations and governments, and in light of individual understanding and perception. Even so, there may have been a form of denial in terms of understanding genocide and the destructive forces of evil. Through hindsight, the concentration camps of Auschwitz, Bergen-Belsen, and Treblinka have become the moral lightening rod of awareness—the epicenter of evil in the modern world. Perhaps Niebuhr had the problem of evil in mind when he penned in the previous poem, "Nothing worth doing can be achieved in our time; therefore we must be saved by hope."

Fifty years later, American society, American Christians, theologians, and students trained in American seminaries continue along a path of denial. September 11, 2001, shook our nation to the core, jarring our sense of security as evil set its jaw squarely in our face. The events at Columbine dashed the illusion that our children were safe in school, while assaults on our churches and courthouses rendered our systems of peace and justice vulnerable. Yet a few sound bites later, we return to our lives, resuming business as usual. The initial awareness does not lead to an assessment of the full impact of evil in our world. We continue along our path of evasion. We fail to name evil—*evil*. We fail to accept its irrefutable power on the self, on society, and particularly on the community known as the body of Christ (Delbanco, p. 197).

What have psychotherapists had to say about the nature of evil? Let's examine the thoughts of five significant psychotherapists on the subject of evil: Erich Fromm, Gerald G. Mays, Karl Menninger, Carl Gustav Jung, and M. Scott Peck.

Chapter 5

Erich Fromm

Erich Fromm, in his book *The Heart of Man: Its Genius for Good and Evil*, approaches the study of evil from the perspective of psychotherapy, becoming one of the first psychotherapists to discuss the nature of evil and the choice to be made between good and evil. He focuses on man's capacity to destroy, his narcissism, and his incestuous fixations. He also writes in a broad sense about independence, the love of life, and overcoming narcissism, which he terms the *syndrome of growth,* as opposed to the *syndrome of decay* (p. 23).

Fromm determined that each person chooses a direction: that of life or death, good or evil, and hatred or love. When Fromm considered the potential for war, specifically nuclear war, he realized psychological analysis could not adequately explain evil. Evil for Fromm is indifference to life. He described the nucleus of mental illness as the seedbed of evil.

For Fromm, evil takes three orientations: Necrophilia—the love of the dead or the love of death; Narcissism—self-love or the preoccupation with oneself to extremes; and Incestuous Ties, which include mother or father fixation, the attachment to family or tribe, and a clinging to the womb to the extent that growth and independence are prevented. Fromm provided us with clear implications. Given our historical vantage point, we can see Hitler as a vivid example of the *syndrome of decay* and the Third Reich as a society turned to evil.

Fromm held to the classic view of man that body and soul, angel and animal belong to two worlds in conflict with each other. Man hungers for unity, oneness, and belonging (p. 117). In Fromm's view, man lives with an internal contradiction. Evil is a human phenomenon in that it seeks to eliminate what is specifically human: reason, love, and freedom. "Evil is man's loss of himself in the tragic attempt to escape the burden of his humanity" (p. 148). The greatest evils are those strivings that are most directed against life: the love of death; the incestuous, symbiotic striving to return to the womb, to the soil, and to the inorganic; and the narcissistic self-immolation that makes man an enemy of life (p. 149).

Fromm recognized that ultimate good is the opponent of idolatry, particularly the idolatry within oneself. When worshipping himself, man becomes an alienated form of humanity, or evil. When man becomes the idol to be worshipped in place of God, he asserts his own omniscience and omnipotence (p. 89–90). Religion acquires the potential, if not guarded, to become a manifestation of group narcissism and thereby motivated by evil. Group narcissism may manifest itself in government, as it clearly did in Nazi Germany; in religious communities, resulting in evil behavior; or in government, with the current Tea Party movement providing a prime example.

A self-proclaimed humanist, Fromm resonates with a profound spirituality when he writes about the good. The ultimate idolatry or the ultimate evil is narcissism in extreme: that is, to reject the good. He cites two examples.

The first example is taken from the familiar Greek legend of Narcissus, the beautiful, young man who fell in love with himself. He rejected the nymph Echo, resulting in her death by a broken heart. His punishment by the god Nemesis caused him to fall in love with his reflection in the water of the lake. In his excitement and admiration of his image, he fell into the water and died. Ultimate idolatry resulted in ultimate evil.

The second example is less extreme, but it is just as poignant because it is so characteristically human. A writer meets a friend and talks to him for a long time about himself. He then says, "I have talked so long about myself, let us now talk about you. How did you like my latest book?" (p. 68–69).

One is reminded of Jesus' conversation with the young ruler whose wealth caused him to lose sight of the good. The implication was to follow the ultimate good as Jesus followed it:

"Good teacher what shall I do to inherit eternal Life," asked the young man?

"Why do you call me good?" Jesus said. "No one is good but God alone. You know the Commandments. You shall not commit adultery. You shall not kill. You shall not steal. You shall not bear false witness. Honor your father and mother," Jesus said.

"All these things, I have done since my youth," replied the young man.

And when Jesus heard it, he said to him. "There is still one thing you are lacking. Sell all you own, and distribute the money to the poor, and you will have treasure in heaven; come and follow me."

—Luke 18:18–22

Erich Fromm's genius for understanding good and evil has relevance for us today (p. 68–69). For Fromm, the fight against idolatry is the fight against narcissism (p. 89). Evil invades the spiritual essence of man, placing his freedom at the crossroads. Goodness is the home that man seeks—it is the sense of union and belonging he needs, and it is the freedom to choose chaos or wholeness that enables man to be human (p. 117). The danger from Fromm's view is not the intrinsic wickedness of man's heart but the inability to wake up to the realistic alternatives and their consequences (p. 141–142).

The recent nuclear disaster in Japan is an example of the choices before us: to curb our appetites for energy consumption and to explore earth-friendly sources of energy or to run the risk of greater nuclear disasters.

In his brilliant analysis, Fromm doesn't seem to cross over to spirituality or religion as some would hope. However, he gets about as close as possible without integrating these worlds. To merge the disciplines, he felt, would be a mistake.

Chapter 6

Gerald G. May

The second psychotherapist of note is Gerald G. May, who draws upon the western and eastern spiritual traditions to help in his psychiatric training and assumptions. This physician/psychiatrist could be considered the father of contemplative psychology—the first to propose and illuminate the psychological experience in light of the spiritual, to say that psychology must make a radical surrender to spirituality. In the book *Will and Spirit: A Contemplative Psychology*, May puts forth the idea of the ultimate surrender of *willfulness* to *willingness*. Willingness for May means a surrendering to the ultimate spirit or deepest level of one's being, in contrast to willfulness, which is an attempt to master, direct, control, or to otherwise manipulate existence (p. 5–6). The latter represents the take-charge part of our lives; the former implies surrender to one's self-separateness and the embracing of mystery. Religion or spirituality helps support and guide this search, despite the inherent tensions between spirituality and psychotherapy.

It is a mistake, May indicates, to ignore the tension between religion and psychotherapy and to fail to acknowledge the inherent weaknesses and strengths of each system. May does not suggest the merging of psychology and spirituality, but he does advocate for "seeing psychological experiences with spiritual eyes" (p. 21).

Psychology, on its own, falls short; it is unable to address the deepest spiritual longings. Only spirituality has the capacity to provide spiritual insight into man's deepest needs. May does not discount the value of giving and receiving psychological help and understanding, but he supports utilizing the energy that the Spirit generates, the life force that keeps us active and dynamic.

From these presuppositions, May describes the foundations for Contemplative Psychology. There are two forms or extremes of spirituality in the mind of May. The first extreme is *affective spirituality*, or emotional spirituality. It might be categorized as a frenetic style of prayer, meditation, or worship. The second form of spirituality, termed *metaphysical*, is focused upon connectional insights and paradoxes. It affirms *mystery* as a given, regardless and independent of emotion. Both extremes run the danger of encouraging narcissism within people or religions. May argues for what he calls a *contemplative style*, one concerned with the essence and source of spirituality. He used the term *intuition* as a kind of specific knowing or perception that is direct and steady, surpassing even reason and inferential thought (p. 25).

May's contemplative style has purity, a direct quality, and a rarity whereby intuition and contemplation are so closely related that they seem to come from the same state of mind or soul (p. 26). It is the purest form of knowing and the realization of one's rootedness in God and creation. This place of knowing is found in the stillness of the mind in silence (p. 27). Contemplative Psychology promotes the search for the mystery of life rather than the assertion of the self. It is to recognize that there is something missing at a soul level. This process is based in solitude and reflection and is often ignored.

May asserts, "Sooner or later a choice will have to be made: to continue a willful positivistic path in which one tries to secure autonomy and self-determination, or to embark on a spiritual path in which one seeks even greater willingness to become a part of the fundamental process of life—in self-surrender" (p. 27).

For May, to know mystery is not to contain it. It is an experience to be felt, enjoyed, or even loved, without being understood. Mystery moves into the fabric of one's life and confronts willfulness.

It tends to make us vulnerable and out of control so that being with mystery requires us to risk and face fear.

Spirit, translated from the Hebrew word *ruah* and the Greek *pneuma* (connoting breath), is the force of *being*, the force of life best understood in relationship, belonging, shared responsibility, and community (p. 33). Spirit is the energy that impels our being and connects us with others in responsive ways, building the avenues to mystery.

Surrender, often described in theology as the "will of God," is seen in the ultimate question addressed to the prophet: "Who will go for us?" The willing servant replies, "Here am I, send me." Surrender represents the total willingness to do the will of mystery. In this use, will responds to mystery; rather than seeking its own power, it bends in humility and obedience. Will's propensity is to expand into willfulness, if it is not governed by love.

May calls *the state of intention* the fundamental essence of the contemplative experience. He refuses to defend or to make sense of it, other than to say it is bedrock, the ground upon which all of life's experience and activities are founded. Perhaps this is what Paul Tillich called "*ground of being*," (emphasis added) where one is captured by a consciousness beyond the individual.

May speaks of *awareness* and *attention*, arguing for what he describes as a *consciousness* that is noticed, recognized, appreciated, or sensed by a person. Awareness is found where one is paying attention, raising consciousness, or expanding consciousness. "Attention is awareness that is focused and sharpened," an openness to allow experiences to occur (p. 47). Ultimately, awareness and attention become one, resulting in moments of unity—or in what some call a peak experience or a religious knowing. The unity experience is often described as being filled with mystery and the inevitable spirituality (p. 51).

May describes this unity experience as "a paradigm for contemplative spirituality" (p. 53). His focus is somewhat different from the charismatic experience of spontaneous healing, prophetic utterance, or the speaking in tongues. May's unity experience is also not a typical intuitive or sixth sense that may be found in a good therapist. He argues for a spirituality developed out of the practice of meditation and quiet prayer. Such practices enable one to "listen with the third ear" (p. 53). For May, spiritual experience is characterized by a loss of self-definition (p. 53). In his unity experience, self-losing is not the exception but fundamental to consciousness, to mystery, and to becoming one with mystery (p. 54). Such an experience of unity occurs when mental activity is suspended and an internal balance or perfection is perceived, resulting in awe, wonder, freedom, warmth, love, truth, and deep recollection of oneness. In his study and work with a wide variety of people, including children, May has been witness to many such experiences.

Unity blossoms in a variety of settings: in nature, in human intimacy, and in common, everyday events; unity is found in music, in poetry, in major life and death encounters, and particularly in religious disciplines of worship—meditation and prayer. What is noteworthy in May's mind is that attempts to achieve unity through drug use and bio feedback are not effective. You simply cannot will a unity experience to happen, you cannot achieve the unity experience—it is a gift of grace from God.

In May's experience, the unity phenomenon has three characteristics. The first is the sense of "being at one" with the universe. Rather than being a self-defining activity, there is a kind of "self-losing" or "self-emptying"—a feeling of belonging to the universe, of being rooted in creation. What is perceived as *me* is suspended; self-identification disappears, even though the physical body-sense is preserved (p. 60).

The second characteristic is a radical change in the level of awareness. The senses are acutely tuned to sensory stimuli, accompanied at times by an element of fear, induced by the loss of control.

The third factor that characterizes the unity experience is a glow, which takes the form of wonder, awe, beauty, reverence, truth, and rightness; a sense of how things really are is clear. While those around the person in his or her moment of epiphany struggle with frustration, he or she clings to the euphoric experience and the promise it holds.

Still, the impact of the unity experience may vary from person to person: expressed in a quick acknowledgement followed by dismissal or resulting in a major life-changing response. Usually it transforms a person's psyche into a healthier, more creative state. In contrast, some may become more willful and self-driven, propelled into a kind of narcissistic self-righteousness. In the worst case, the experience might result in a paranoid grandiosity, where one is convinced he or she has been chosen to accomplish some grand feat in the world. For most, the response to a unity experience is one of "letting be, resting and accepting, finding peace, or surrendering" (p. 64). There is a sense of returning home after a long separation.

Unity experiences are sacred; they cannot be made to happen, nor can they be characterized as something we do but rather as something that is given to us. This something is grace. The experience points to mystery rather than a tidy definition; the experience is a river that cannot be contained. The key is a willingness to permit the experience to happen (p. 67). May's major contribution is his clear distinction between willfulness and willingness: the desire to control contrasted with the desire to surrender.

The spiritual quest takes on three basic dimensions: a desire for unconditional love, a need for belonging and union, and a deep hunger to "just be" (p. 13). May describes unconditional love as a desire to be in love with life itself, with the creation, with the universe, and with God. He senses a kind of hunger deep within the human psyche, which not only wants to love God but also to receive God's love (p. 13).

The need to belong and to find union is the most difficult; although, some religious practices provide assistance and structure. May recognized that the need to belong, the need to love, and the need to be loved are almost inseparable (p. 82), seemingly progressing from child-like dimensions to a larger, more universal consciousness, a love that grows in depth and maturity as it is given and received (p. 85). To "just be" is the fundamental need to be accepted as we are. It is as if, in some unexplained way, we are in love—enveloped in love, and in that brief moment, God smiles. May rightly perceives that the deep, spiritual longing and the search to find one's roots, one's origin in the Creator, to be part of the whole, is everyone's search to overcome separateness. Psychology can assist and help in a person's confusion, but only religion speaks with historical knowledge, wisdom, and the authority of God and then descriptively as God is perceived and known (p. 88).

May turns from the spiritual quest to the "issue of the shadow sides" of spirituality. How can spiritual longing, for example, turn against itself and become twisted into destructiveness and evil? Why is it that the profound need for unconditional love, for union to roots, and for belonging becomes such a threat to self-image? (p. 92)

For May, the answer is in the responsibility to face the truth of one's less-than-acceptable nature and the courage required to face the necessary changes in the self-image. Resistance to truth, efforts to keep secrets hidden, and reluctance to change behavior are all familiar reactions by a patient under psychoanalysis. The key catalyst for change is the unity experience, the acknowledgement of self-truth. Reconciliation and willingness to surrender to the divine will signal a return to authenticity—that place where the image of the self, or the dying belief in the image of self, is joined with the dying of one's image of the world (p. 92).

The spiritual journey is difficult, according to May, just as the therapeutic process is difficult. Care, nurture, and mentoring in the spiritual journey are not mentioned by May; although, one senses the process requires a kindness and balance such as is required in psychotherapy. The duality of self and the world is a constant, making the spiritual search very difficult (p. 104). May's concern is that the self-proclaiming ego tends to fight the unity experience and hinder the process of unity realization to the point that "self-image and unity experiences are mortal enemies" (p. 112).

May notes that the backlash and the danger to the spiritual journey stems from spiritual narcissism. He defines spiritual narcissism as the unconscious use of spiritual practices and the experience, or insight, to increase self-importance; in other words, trying to identify with an image of goodness, holiness, or specialness instead of a journey of humility and self-sacrifice. If pushed far enough, the narcissism becomes a self-motivator and the producer of religious willfulness and pride. Thus, the energy to come to God and connect to God comes from the self rather than as an invitation from the sacred. May describes narcissism in the religious context:

> Spiritual narcissism can be seen in one form or another at the core of virtually all forms of religious distortion or excess, from individuals who avoid responsibility by escaping into prayer and meditation, to the cult that pulls young adults into glass-eye automatism, to Bible-thumping Christian groups who seek material wealth and political power in the name of Jesus, to the "inquisitions" and "holy wars" that kill the children of creation in the name of the creator of us all. Spiritual narcissism as a condition arises whenever one uses one's faith to accomplish one's personal aims. It is the absolute opposite of true spirituality, in which one allows oneself to be used by one's faith to accomplish the will of God. (p. 119)

May does not identify at this point in his analysis the subject of evil; however, as noted above, the world's most grotesque evils have been committed "in the service of God" (p. 119–120). Extreme forms of willfulness may well become evil or motivated by evil and said to be in the name of God.

May defines the concepts of *good* and *evil* in the context of unity and duality. He begins by making friends with *mystery*. In fact, he embraces mystery, defining the good in mystery as a connection to the divine and personal surrender of man as friendship with the divine. Personal surrender is equated with "coming home." God is thus defined as the ultimate good, the ultimate mystery, and the ultimate, benevolent source of energy or life force.

May qualifies his perception of mystery as also having elements that are not good. In May's mind, there is a psychic force that is basically malevolent. It is called *evil* or *demonic*. Evil impels or compels us away from union with the good in mystery. Evil gives impetus to willfulness and subverts man's surrender to good in mystery. Evil is an energy that drives or pulls man away from the mystery of good. It is a force that seductively leads people into habitual willfulness and self-importance. Evil takes form in rebellion, seduction, fascination, and fear. Unfortunately, evil is too often ignored as irrelevant. Even May's attitude would suggest that evil is insignificant. One wonders if May has underestimated the potential of evil to bring harm to the human psyche, society, and ultimately, to the cosmos.

Perhaps, from the clinical perception, evil is seen as a force either in the mind, society, or the cosmos that operates as energy or power, somehow held in balance by mystery. But May is unclear. He does acknowledge that evil has the capacity to "alter radically the deepest levels of human functioning and experience" (p. 247). He identifies five discrete visions of evil as demonic:

1. The traditional, psychological view of evil as a force that is a psychological phenomenon that takes the form of pure symbolism and as a category to describe the working within the mind
2. The archetypal view of evil as a collective, unconscious manifestation in symbol
3. The existential view, as expressed whenever anything other than God becomes the object of one's ultimate concern
4. The monistic view of evil as illusionary, i.e., to give evil or the demonic credence is to engage in illusion
5. The dualistic view of evil as real; good and evil are vitally engaged in a struggle for dominance and destruction of life.

In summary, May views evil as present when anything other than mystery and the love of God become our ultimate concern (p. 249). May's focus is upon the contemplative search for unity, with the ultimate test being the good. The pathway for such a journey is to surrender to mystery; although, increased guidance is needed along the way. He notes that psychotherapy's primary concern is to move one toward increased autonomy and independence. Such a contrast between the disciplines results in paradox and dualism. Overlooked or minimized, one is forced into a tension where rules, judgments, discrimination, and a confrontation between good and evil are the norm. Unfortunately, the human being will vacillate between the desire for a unity experience and independence, even to the point where one may feel the vacillation between two different universes or realities (p. 260–261). Such a view, as May notes, is not only achieved in the man, Jesus, who testified of being both human and divine, but also, potentially, in every human being.

Something should be said about May's view of energy as a basic life force within the physical bodies of people, in all forms and patterns of dynamic relationships, and in all matter in the universe (p. 174). This is contrasted to western thought, in which psychic energy is generated within and limited to the human mind and body. It is May's conviction that such energy is rooted in the *good* or *agape love*. For May, this is an attractive proposition that in some form explains the energy not only within human beings but also within the universe (p. 172). From such a proposition, May argues that "basic life energy and divine love are so intimately related as to be essentially inseparable" (p. 202). He notes that all spiritual traditions are filled with images that attempt to capture the message of creative energy—water, fire, light, and breath all describe such a symbolic message. In short, the contemplative vision is based on the fundamental idea that the life force of creation is an expression of divine love and an appreciation of life itself in all its forms (p. 204).

The final category in May's foundations of contemporary psychology is the encounter with evil. In May's opinion, acts of vengeance, envy, or other destructive motivations are evil. Evil is malevolent intent! The intent to harm is the human side of evil and differs from sin, which may be a well-intended but misguided action. To put it another way, both sin and evil involve a distinctive separation of a person from God and from others. In sin, the separation may be a mistake or omission; whereas, evil intends separation. Vengeance, for example, becomes visible as human evil because it serves to increase separateness, willfulness, and alienation. It always attacks our willingness to surrender. It hampers human desire to find the divine, to welcome unity and love. It stands in direct opposition to agape love and reconciliation (p. 267).

May argues with persuasive perception that if we want to do wrong, and do the worst we can, then evil enters, and increased alienation, growing resentment, and destructive willfulness erode our capacity to love or be loved (p. 268). It is a moot question whether one considers evil as symbolic or real when faced with the horrors of genocide, the shock of 9-11, or the pain of estrangement (p. 272).

Avoidance or ignorance of the subject of evil can no longer be an adequate answer or response. Evil is not something for fascination; it has the capacity to influence nature and consciousness in deeply subtle yet malignant ways. It is nameless, but it can be felt and perceived directly and indirectly (p. 273). There is a coldness and a harshness to it, an absence of love that generates fear. Only through trust in the divine, or God, can one reduce evil's impact. Support comes from community, friends, guides, Scripture, and openness in prayer. Strength comes from our dependency upon each other in God, upon God in each other, and upon the transcendent God in whose image we are made (p. 276).

May sums up his thoughts with these words:

> I do not know what is ultimately good or evil, not even what is real or unreal. But I do know that there is no way I can precede upon my own personal resources. In this as in all things, I am utterly and irrevocably dependent upon a power that I can in no way objectify. I call this power God, and God is beyond my understanding, beyond good and evil, beyond doubt and trust, beyond even life and death. God's love and power and spirit exist in me, through me, and in all creatures. But God is unimaginably beyond all this as well. I also know that in my heart I wish to do and be what God would desire of me. Therefore, in humility and fear, I give myself; I commit my soul to God, the One Almighty Creator, and the Ultimate Source of reality. Good or bad, right or wrong, these things are beyond me. I love, but I do not know. I live and act and decide between this and that as best I can, but ultimately, I do not know. And thus I say, in the burning vibrancy of your love and terror, "Thy will be done." (p. 277)

Chapter 7

Karl Menninger

Karl Menninger, psychiatrist and psychoanalyst, when writing *Whatever Became of Sin?* was convinced that our nation and society was slowly slipping into a sickness of the spirit. The sickness was characterized by a posture of apathy and accompanied by the somatic and psychological signs or *sins of acedia* (unresponsiveness, boredom, laziness). In Menninger's mind, the result was a society filled with fear, self-rejection, and self-confusion (p. 6). Simply stated, acedia manifests itself in attitudes of "non-caring." Acedia is the great sin of indifference. It is at the heart of all sin. It has many names: pride, selfishness, alienation. In some circles acedia may be labeled mental illness, while in other circles, acedia may be viewed as estrangement and separation from self and God (p. 146).

Menninger put forth his thesis that modern man and culture had lost a sense of sin and was avoiding the use of the word. He explains that in doing so, modern man has shifted his responsibility for evil into a kind of limbo of avoidance. The result may well be a rejection of all that is psychic and religious.

For Menninger, there is a compulsion to rediscover the meaning of sin and its counterpart, grace. He writes about collective sin, about sin with all its darkness; he explains and explores the impact of sin; he identifies sin, the deadly and not so deadly varieties. He describes the power of intent, of neglect, and attitudes of the heart linked to sin. The consequences of sin are self-destruction and ultimate death (p. 172).

Menninger wants to awaken and revive the concept and belief in personal responsibility so that the word *sin* has value and to reestablish the understanding that sin is something to be avoided and eliminated (p. 189–190). Only then can amends, restitution, and acknowledgement become a resource to restoration from the consequences of sin. The concept of sin applies to all vocations and to the ultimate healing of a society. He begins with religious leaders and their communities, but he does not limit his discussion to the religious world. He touches all vocations, including medical doctors and psychiatrists, in particular. All are responsible for taking seriously injustice, crime, and the deadly sins of the society.

It is disheartening to read Menninger and to conclude that, forty years later, he is closer to the truth today than when he wrote his book. It may be revealing to note the title to his last chapter, "The Bluebird on the Dung Heap," suggesting that humanity, in its struggles and suffering, is more important than its successes. To recognize the poor and the hardships in life and still to hold on to God, even when God may be silent or absent, is to find a bluebird in the midst of suffering. As any farm boy knows, that is where chickens reside! To say God is a bluebird and our world is a dung heap may not be an overstatement. It may well be the simplest symbol of grace, that is, if you believe in bluebirds sitting on dung heaps.

In summary, Menninger believes that the disappearance of sin involves a shift in the responsibility for evil (p. 179), the qualities of which are aggression and self-destruction (p. 117). Unfortunately, the intrinsic antagonism between "soul doctors" and "mind doctors" has caused this chasm to become even larger, and unless there is an awakening, the separation may not be appreciated nor the dangers faced by our society.

Behind all of the inquiries lies what Menninger calls a wishful, fearful, existential terror that threatens the bulwarks of the good life. The good life may be swept away by unmitigated, uncontrolled sin

(p. 187–188). "The evil," says Menninger, "seems to be coming from outside us, from others, from another being similar to ourselves but more alienated" (p. 187). He implies that the identification of evil is a dead argument and that sin, classified, faced, acknowledged, and forgiven, is the only way that health and well-being, for the individual and the culture, can be restored. Otherwise, without responsible lives lived, this "vague amorphous evil" appears all about us in awful happenings and terrible, wretched circumstances (p. 188). The most adequate answer is grace—God's grace, which faces the human predicament and longs for restoration and reconciliation of man.

Chapter 8

Carl Jung

The study of psychology began in most minds with Sigmund Freud and Carl Jung, but only Jung, to my knowledge, writes about God, his own inner development, and the unconscious in terms of the religious. He did so in his last published book before his death: *Memories, Dreams, Reflections.*

To Jung, the psyche was a profound reality. The spiritual essence of life was the ultimate focus of his existence (Jung, p. 8). His autobiography was first and foremost a record of his religious ideas and his treatment of religion, particularly his views on the problem of evil and of a God who was not always good or kind (p. 10). However, Jung was explicitly committed to Christianity and the problems faced by the Christian (p. xi). His faith was one of the essential features of his life. He wrote to a young clergyman in 1952, "I find that all my thoughts circle around God like the planets around the sun, and are as irresistibly attracted by Him. I would feel it to be the grossest sin if I were to oppose any resistance to this force" (p. xi).

Only in this one book does Jung speak about God and his personal experience of God, and in doing so, he attempts to separate his objective search, which he describes as the scientific inquiry, from his subjective, inner experience. As a scientist, he is an empiricist. When he writes subjectively, he assumes such experiences can be verified only in terms of similarity with, and mutuality of, experiences held in common. To understand Jung's insights into the psyche, it is necessary to understand and reflect upon the demands of living in paradox, balancing faith and reason.

Jung was convinced that the Christian myth, which he describes as storytelling, needed to be developed in every generation so that it took new forms of understanding. He described the outpouring of the Holy Spirit upon the apostles, whereby they became "Sons of God." He saw son-ship as the root of wholeness and a way of living connected to God. In his mind, this was a myth of self-realization, of "God incarnate," first in the man Jesus and secondly in the development of the intuitive image of "Christ within us" as human beings.

The development of the Christian myth continued unchallenged for the first millennium (p. 328). It was not until the second millennium that man became incensed with "Hubris of Consciousness," the idea that nothing is greater than man and his deeds so that the Christian myth was no longer viable and wholeness was sought elsewhere. The Hubris view developed into the twentieth century and even to this day, because the Christian myth was lost. The result was confrontation of the Christian world by evil in the form of naked injustice, tyranny, lies, slavery, and coercion of the conscience.

The manifestation of evil in Germany and Russia clearly persists today in many parts of Africa. Many post-colonial nations are ruled by totally corrupt people who exploit their countries without conscience or limit. Genocide, enslavement, and persistent famine characterize so much of that continent.

For Jung, the manifestation of evil, which first erupted in Germany, was later clearly observed in permanent form in the Russian nation. Evil then undermined Christianity and became a determined reality to be faced. It is a reality whose power presents grave peril to the disoriented person (p. 329). Jung suggests that evil is addressed first and foremost by facing "the self" and acknowledging the human and divine within man. So to live without self-deception or self-delusion becomes of prime importance in dealing with evil. In Jung's mind, such orientation is necessary to understand the phenomenon of evil as it manifests itself in governments, nations, and religious institutions. To deny the reality of evil is to ignore the ultimate message of religion. But the implication is the necessity for "self knowledge" as the refocused myth and story of the Christian faith. The development of the message and the myth is essential. Myth, in Jung's mind, is no more than telling stories in which a person describes the psychic life in which emotions are healed and strength is given (p. 300). Hints of such strength come from the unconscious, in dreams and figurative illusions, and even in foreknowledge (p. 302–303).

Jung senses not only for his day but also for the present time, a deep need for reorientation of the psychic world in which spiritual care has been so powerful and healing. Unfortunately, modern man is lopsided and distorted by his limited understanding of the self, particularly of the subconscious (p. 331). Jung laments:

> We stand face to face with the terrible question of evil and do not even know what is before us, let alone what to pit against it. And even if we did know, we still could not understand how it could happen here. With glorious naiveté a statesmen comes out with the proud declaration that he has no "imagination for evil." Quite right, we have no imagination for evil, but evil has us in its grip. Some do not want to know this, and others are identified with evil; that is the psychological situation in the world today. Some call themselves Christian and imagine that they can trample so-called evil underfoot, by merely willing it. Others have succumbed to it and no longer see the good. Evil today has become a visible great power. One half of humanity believes and grows strong on a doctrine fabricated by human ratiocination. The other half sickens from the lack of myth commensurate with the situation. The Christian nations have come to a sorry pass; Christianity slumbers and has neglected to develop the myth further in the course of the centuries. (p. 331)

Jung's basic question posed by the early Gnostics, "Whence comes evil?" remains unanswered. Jung explains, "We stand empty-handed and bewildered primarily as the result of the political situations and a science whose trumpets have ignored the since-forgotten soul of man" (p. 332–333). The hope, Jung suggests, lies with the outpouring of God's Spirit, willing mankind to become "Sons of God." For Jung, wholeness was to be achieved and developed through the power of symbols. He sees the mandala as a representation of the unconscious self and believes that his paintings of mandalas help him identify emotional disorders and work toward wholeness or integration of the personality (p. 334).

Jung sees God as one who wishes to become man. God wants to empty himself (Phil. 2:7) in order to enter into the human dilemma, into ordinary human existence in order to save man. Jung realizes there are contradictions and inconsistencies; nonetheless, room is made to allow the one God to grant wholeness and synthesis of opposites. Jung explains this in symbols. It is a fact, he asserts, "Symbols, by their very nature, can so unite the opposites that these no longer diverge or clash, but mutually supplement one another and give meaningful shape to life" (p. 338).

What Jung suggests is profound. When symbols are defined descriptively, they gain the ability to bridge the differences in opposite perceptions. Imagination helps to observe more than one meaning or to conceive of more than one reality. Divergent understandings can co-exist, supplementing one another and giving deeper meaning to life and spirituality.

Chapter 9

M. Scott Peck

M. Scott Peck opened the minds and hearts of the American church and interested bystanders with his first book, *The Road Less Traveled*. He encouraged a whole generation of clergy and lay people to understand the depth and the consequences of their work and the need to support their mutual disciplines. His courage to write and the brilliance to clarify issues indeed makes "all the difference," to use Robert Frost's words, from his poem, *The Road Not Taken*. It is literally a road less traveled for the psychiatrist, analyst, and clergy person. He has given us hope; although, he may be a voice in the wilderness, crying out for a sense of reality for both disciplines. Peck, in his first book, calls for a new psychology of love, which affirms traditional values and encourages spiritual growth. His premise is that life is difficult and an unending journey toward spiritual awareness. It is a search for identity and self-awareness.

His second book, a companion volume, *The People of the Lie*, was published five years later, in 1983. Peck used the same method to probe the essence of evil with the hope of healing humanity from its effects. Evil is a difficult and resistant subject, but Peck's contribution, according to Harvey Cox, renowned theologian and best-selling author, may have begun a new conversation between religion and psychology with a new and firm voice.

Ten years later, Peck wrote his next significant book, *Further Along the Road Less Traveled,* in which he continues to explore self-identity with greater depth. He suggests that life is complex and that we choose our own pathway through life. Our journey can make the difference. The road is not paved, nor is it brightly lit; road-signs are absent, and the pathway is rocky. The road has the quality of a wilderness, unfolding and dynamic. Peck describes this search for identity and wholeness as a "concentric circle" that is expanding from its beginning, much like the rings in a pond that expand when a stone is thrown into it. In short, the journey is neither simple nor straightforward.

Norman MacLean, author of *Young Men and Fire* and *A River Runs Through It*, also expressed the notion that the search for identity is continuous. "The problem of self-identity is not just a problem for the young. It is a problem all the time; perhaps 'the problem.' It haunts old age, and when it no longer does, it should tell you, you are already dead" (p. xiii). This notion of an ongoing process may be applied to our identity as Christians and to the unfolding identity of Christianity.

Each of Peck's books contributes to the discussion between religion and psychology; however, *People of the Lie* may break new ground as most writers continue to ignore conversations about evil. It is upon this subject and this volume that my discussion will center, for it may help focus upon identity—Christian identity, church identity, and community vitality.

Peck's first words, like those of Gerald G. May, state that the subject of evil is dangerous, a subject to be handled with care. Evil is not an abstraction but alive. The struggle to bring healing, particularly to transform evil nature, begins in self-reflection. Facing one's own humanity, in an attitude of confession, is the first defense and the primary source of strength in dealing with evil. The second is one's spirituality; although, Peck only implies as much and makes a strong effort to separate the practice of healing and science from religion. What he does pursue, however, is the cornerstone of psychotherapy—a willingness to take an honest and accurate view of the self (p. 12).

Peck's methods are direct observation and reflection upon case studies. The process, admittedly, leans toward the psychology of evil. Note that the subject of evil was absent in his training as a psychiatrist, and until he addressed it, the subject was also largely ignored in the field of psychiatry (p. 40). In fact, religion and science were incompatible in his training, and any discussion between the two was rejected. The separation of science and religion was a mistake, he felt, particularly concerning the discussion of human evil. It was Peck's observation that the psychiatric world has approached the psyche too readily from the scientific or "left brain perspective," while religion, on the other hand, has leaned more toward "right brain exploration and training" (p.41). In the case of evil, religious training was more apt to grope about, exploring the subject of evil through intuition, feelings, faith, and revelation. What Peck doesn't sense is that evil is a vast mystery in both disciplines and difficult to separate and identify.

Peck begins his discussion by defining evil as a force that resides either inside or outside of human beings and seeks to kill life. He defines goodness, the opposite of evil, as the mystery that promotes life. The complexity of the human condition is a result of the tension between good and evil. Spirituality is routinely ignored and avoided in the medical world, making an understanding of evil incomplete. Peck assumes, rightly, that one can only approach human evil in terms of healing a human psyche based upon the force of ultimate good, which is God's love manifested in the healer.

One wonders in what way one's spirituality becomes the energy or force to identify and confront evil with. From Peck's experience in the clinical setting, evil promotes deep feelings of revulsion in the healer, signaling danger. Evil rejects health and is bent on destruction. It is wise, in Peck's opinion, for a person to avoid and withdraw at that point, as most psychiatrists do, feeling the danger and unable to identify the cause of the revulsion.

Peck's observations are helpful, for they identify evil as a force that engenders confusion. Lies are intended to confuse. People whose lives are based upon lies and deception are dangerous, promoting pain and suffering. Bernard Madoff, the self-confessed author of the biggest financial swindle in history, called by US District Court Judge Denny Chin an "extraordinary evil fraud," in the Wall Street Journal, confirms Peck's point (p. 1). Unfortunately, one wonders if redemption is possible when one considers the deception and tragedy suffered by so many as a result of Madoff's actions and the actions of other anonymous Wall Street architects of the *Mortgage Bubble*.

It is noteworthy that Peck approaches the dangers of evil with compassion and love. It is his method of healing wherever possible that helps remind us that the human condition, its failures and redemption, always lies in the hands of the divine. Pride, arrogance, and laziness, or the desire to escape legitimate suffering, are the quickest ways for evil to reach the heart of man, whether that of the cleric, therapist, or patient. Assigning scapegoats, transference, projection, and creating triangles by diverting conflict between two people onto a third are all methods that reside in the devil's toolbox. Each defense is dedicated to preserving the self-image of perfection (p. 75). Such defense works to maintain "self-image," whether it is moral or otherwise. "Image, appearance, [and] outward standing" are keys to the defense as evil appears in people (p. 76). It is the pretense that counts, almost to the point that weakness or confession is ignored. Self-deceit is the major component of evil. Examination is intolerable. Evil hates insight and goodness because goodness and insight penetrate deception.

In Peck's opinion, there is a particular variety of narcissism that may be considered evil. Self-absorption takes on many forms from childhood to adulthood and can be normal, but one variant is pathological. He agrees with Eric Fromm, calling evil "malignant narcissism" (p.78).

Evil is Gerald May's characterization of the uncommitted will in his book *Will and Spirit* (p. 287). Such a person refuses to recognize the divine, be it God, the ultimate mystery, or the ultimate good. The same person can be extraordinarily willful and seek high levels of control to achieve the aim he or she seeks.

Peck builds on Gerald May's categories of *willingness* and *willfulness*. The former is described as a willful surrender to the divine; the latter is expressed in the desire to be "the king of the universe." In Peck's mind, pride meshed with self-image to the extent of self-worship inordinately results in malignant human evil and may be more common than we realize.

Human will is a category filled with paradox, no matter how one attempts to identify and describe it. The genesis of its origin is difficult to grasp and explain. There is one clear indicator of evil's nature: there is no neutral ground. "You can run, but you can't hide!" The force of evil is real and alive, and it will always attempt to engage the will of a human being. It is equally true that the force of good is valiant and powerful and seeks to win man's will as well. From my observations, I think the defeats seem to take their toll, especially if one has any degree of perception and awareness. Too little has been written on or taken seriously about the matter of evil within the thinking Protestant world, and the matters of grace and forgiveness have been minimized in the secular arena.

Peck argues that one should hesitate to regard evil as an illness because too little study has been done and there has been too little observation to understand its cure. Peck writes that there is the danger of evil evoking anger, disgust, and even hate. In his mind, the healer's primary energy must be love and compassion.

In contrast, from the religious perspective, Jesus' confrontation with evil was always direct, with the exception of his succumbing to the crucifixion. Peck's caution may be a state of ignorance and helplessness toward identifying evil. Little is written in terms of the psychology of evil. If evil is an illness, then the doctor and pastor may be best equipped to give care with love and insight; to observe human evil within the community and to observe its power to destroy leadership and religious faith may be another set of issues.

Peck shifts his focus to possession, with its many faces, writing with humility in the search for truth. He is convinced from his practice that evil has been the cause of mental illness in specific cases where no other diagnosis was plausible. His thesis, which may be as strange to the mental health community as it is to the religious sphere, is that the demonic and the satanic manifest themselves in lies and illusions, embodying the spirit of mental illness. He calls Satan the Father of Lies and defines good mental health as "an on-going process dedicated to reality at all costs" (p. 207). The implication is that good spirituality is equally committed to reality and a bridge to the divine, where the spirits of love and surrender are understood.

Peck bases his analysis of evil and the use of exorcism on two cases of demonic possession that he witnessed firsthand. He was a part of a team that supported an exorcist, faced the demonic, and successfully removed vile spirits from two patients who sought help.

For Peck, evil is not an abstraction; it is real; the demonic, satanic, human form is tangible and dangerous. He implies a similarity between demon possession and mental illness, following a common thread between exorcism and the scientific process of psychotherapy with one major difference: the use of power.

Psychotherapy, generally, does not rely on power. The therapist, rather, defers to the patient, guiding his or her client to confront issues and, like a surgeon, targets the underlying problem. If successful, the malignancy is removed and health is restored (p. 186–187).

Emotional surgery of any kind runs the danger of "brain washing" and could compromise the integrity of the individual. The fact that one of his patients who was undergoing an exorcism felt relief, then gratefulness, followed by feelings of being "raped" is a deep concern. In Peck's mind, the exorcism was justified when "informed consent" was given. Yet, there is a doubt. What safeguards were used? What kind of coercion can be justified by love? Methods of healing do matter. Ethics are essential.

It would be easy to dismiss Peck at this point, and I expect many do. However, on further examination, his observations, findings, and follow-up treatments have a ring of validity and seem worth examining, as so few in his profession are willing to understand or write about the subject of evil. Peck's training, his attention to detail, and his search for truth are worth noting, despite the primitive nature of the exorcism.

Peck describes exorcism as a kind of brain surgery in which God or Christ is the surgeon charged with expelling evil. Free will (signed consent, if you will) is essential; although, emotional coercion seems to be used to confront the lies, untruth, or false realities. Values are confronted directly, and distorted truths are exposed. Fear is removed by love; yet Peck provides no details to describe what exorcism does or how it is applied. There are too many questions left unanswered.

Peck describes evil, the demonic or satanic, as he observed it during treatment and as the evil was expelled. He determined that evil has the following characteristics:

1. Satan or evil, Lucifer or the demonic, are forces whose rebellion is primarily against the divine and life of the divine in mankind. Evil may be or not be redeemable.
2. Evil is out to destroy the mystical good or spirit of good. He is the spirit that opposes any form of good manifested in human form.
3. He is limited to the human body and has no power except in the human body.
4. His presence is identified in people of the lie. His presence is based upon deception and illusion.
5. Evil's power is focused upon human weakness (greed, pride); his weapons are fear and distorted reality.
6. His presence, once revealed, is hateful and takes on the energy of hate.
7. Evil will also take the form of deception and hide its own reality from the human mind.
8. Evil has one weakness. It is a "show off" and will go to extraordinary levels to gain attention. Pride and narcissism are at the root of this weakness.

Peck's concern is the need for a shift in American psychiatry to recognize the issues of spirituality that are not only neglected but also actively ignored.

Paul Tournier, a distinguished Swiss physician and psychiatrist, also decried the divorce of science and religion in the treatment of mental illness. He tells the story of a clergyman and a psychiatrist who are walking down the same street on the opposite sides. They tip their hats and go their separate ways. In both cases, neither attempts to relate. They further ignore and reject their respective disciplines. The trust and respect of their disciplines have either been denigrated, or they have never found a basis for common respect. Unfortunately, there is a great need for both to stop in their paths and cross the street and greet each other as healers and priests, both of whom are deeply needed in today's world.

Each of these experts offers a partial glimpse at what lies behind the mask of evil. Erich Fromm focused on man's capacity to destroy, his narcissism, and his incestuous fixations. With Gerald May's contemplative psychology, we learned how *willfulness*, marked by unrelenting self-determination, may contribute to evil action. Karl Menninger wrote about the sickness of the spirit. He described evil as deep-seated apathy and a refusal to assume responsibility. Karl Jung, bridging religion and psychology, approached the subject of evil through his understanding of God, his own inner development and the world of the unconscious. His identification of evil during the Second World War and of evil's manifestation in institutions, whether political or religious, was extremely helpful. Finally, M. Scott Peck described his experience of evil through his practice of medicine. His case studies point to the beginning of evil's identification and to the exorcism of evil.

In the next chapter, we turn our focus to the unmasking of evil. Exposing evil may well be the most significant paradigm shift in the church since the Reformation, and it is extremely needed in our time.

Part 3
Evil Unmasked—Theological Perspective

Chapter 10

G. Lloyd Rediger

There are two equal and opposite errors into which our race can fall about the devils. One is to disbelieve in their existence. The other is to believe, and to feel an excessive and unhealthy interest in them. They themselves are equally pleased by both errors and hail a materialist or a magician with the same delight (p. ix).

—C.S. Lewis
The Screwtape Letters

Just as C.S. Lewis once warned of Satan's undermining work within the church, G. Lloyd Rediger, in *Clergy Killers*, addresses the phenomenon of leadership and church community abuse, providing guidance for pastors and church congregations under attack. Evil is serious business, and to ignore its impact upon clergy, laity, or the community of God's people invites abuse. The behavior of people motivated by evil and the results of systems torn apart are easily identified by examining the footprints left behind. Rediger delineates six imprints of evil (p. 9):

1. It is distinctive and intentional.
2. It is determined, and it doesn't stop.
3. It is deceitful and lives on falsehood and lies.
4. It is demonic and enjoys disorder and creates chaos.
5. It reacts in denial and illusion.
6. It is confronted best by discernment based upon intuition and enlightenment.

"Facing evil must be exercised as carefully and as skillfully as possible," argues Rediger. Pastors need to take time to learn these lessons, especially when they have been trained to be open and to share leadership based upon mutual trust. Time must be set aside to explore pathways within the parish for connecting and listening. An intentional system of procedures needs to be in place that involves the entire staff in planning and problem solving. Evil conceals itself in the back room of gossip and slander, where it initiates its character attacks. Without training and systems in place to quickly address dissension, the pastoral leadership is vulnerable to attacks.

The pastor and parish are often unaware of the danger lurking in their midst. The naiveté of well-intentioned members of the Christian community is profound. Abusive people typically hide in cloaks of piety and social acceptability and are viewed by others as valued, good people. The defense against their attacks is a savvy laity, with the ability and skills to "street fight," to recognize the potential abuse or disorder and translate that knowledge into community action. The explosive nature of abuse and the persistence of those committed and motivated to abuse can be underestimated and left unaddressed. The major defense against abuse is the training and empowering of the lay leadership. Lay leaders need to be sensitized to the potential of evil and people motivated by evil. Their watchfulness is the first line of defense.

Clergy Abuse

Rediger's contribution is in identifying the growing phenomenon of clergy abuse and the tendency to ignore or blame the dysfunction on something else. It is easy to look back at my parish experiences and remember articulate people who enjoyed community support and in parking lot conversations undermined the church leaders. If ignored, these behaviors may and do destroy the sacred trust given to the church.

It is clear that the phenomenon of clergy abuse is on the increase. One major denomination reported informally that 2,500 of their pastors had been forced out of their congregations in the year Rediger was writing. It is my observation that more and more young pastors reflect mistrust and harbor a bunker mentality where trust and openness are absent. More and more judiciary work is being tied up with issues of abuse to leadership and communities. Ignored by some, the abuse goes underground, and ultimately, the community either falls apart, dies, or is rendered ineffective. The answer, as already noted, is training: development of responsible leaders who make effective use of polity and accountability, conflict management, the nurturing of spiritual disciples, and the establishment of boundaries.

"Loose cannons" and "attitude-challenged malcontents" must be dealt with at whatever level needed. In short, abusive behaviors of any type have a way of undermining the health of the congregation. Only healthy, enlightened, well-trained leadership can face issues that threaten congregational life and well-being (p. 23).

Normal Conflict

Rediger raises the question, "Is conflict in the church normal?" While conflict may be normal in some cases, incivility and abuse are not acceptable (p. 47). Thriving communities find conflict to be healthy because it keeps communication open, promotes authenticity, honors diversity, teaches creativity, and generates respect. But conflict, unmanaged and not addressed, can be dangerous and destructive. Ignoring dissension drives conflict underground, where it gathers strength and momentum. A few generalizations are worth noting in terms of the dangers. According to Rediger:

1. Conflict requires energy, and its response must be managed carefully.
2. Negative energy is more commonly expressed today, and there is a greater willingness to hold leadership accountable.
3. Conflict is real and sometimes mean-spirited.
4. Conflict can escalate into abuse if not managed judiciously.
5. Effective conflict management is not the norm in church communities or in judicatories.

Dissension, vindictiveness, and abuse in congregations are on the rise, and the willingness of many religious leaders (clergy and laity) to cleanse and destroy careers and congregations is frightening. The result is the "clergy killer" phenomenon.

Rediger affirms the normalcy of community conflict; church dissension has been a reality since the birth of the church. What he notes, however, is the increased frequency and intensity of the conflict experienced today. There is a deep desire within the theological movement to move toward conformity in belief and practice. The result is a kind of theological cleansing and a platform for clergy killers to stage a movement with greater potential for conflict and abuse. Conflict is further escalated by "infrastructure collapse." Family-connected networks, the strength of congregations in the past, no longer have the extended connections that they once had. Established systems suffer, leaving the door open to the misuse of power. With increased diversity of the congregants, developing consensus within the community becomes problematic. Discontent is born and seeks nourishment, eating away at the framework of the institution.

Rediger notes that part of the infrastructure collapse is due to the new culture of adolescents that resists the experience, wisdom, and practices of older generations. Pushed far enough, this disparity has the potential to generate anger and distrust across generational lines. Worship styles, appropriate dress, and behavior often become points of dissension. This phenomenon is not a new one, but it may be accelerated like other aspects of our fast-paced culture. The result is abuse on the part of each, minimizing sacred trust and polarizing worship into a battle of generations. What is needed are wise, patient, and sensitive leaders, both pastoral and laity, keeping a balance of love and responsibility for the total community. Training is essential. Expectations need to be clearly made and enforced; trust and responsibility by both clergy and laity need to be clearly practiced and understood.

I would add that efforts to involve children in the worship service raises some eyebrows. The movement to provide children's sermons and to involve children in the sacraments exposes their behaviors to the disapproving eyes of older generations. Silent prayer is no longer so silent, and while some welcome the sound of children, others still believe children should be managed carefully.

Rediger describes the "melting pot society" that is the church. Cultural differences and preferences that are not identified and honored trigger an unhealthy climate in any community. The church isn't exempt. The conflict generated is characterized by violated expectations, which induce anger and result in chaos. When healthy management models, which incorporate listening, communicating, and consensus building, are absent, incivility and mean-spiritedness ensue, and the peace and unity of the community is threatened (p. 50–58).

Spiritual Conflict: The Power of Evil

Rediger focuses upon the abnormal conflicts that are a part of some communities. It is to the abnormal reality, the power of evil and its intentionality, its unhealthy and often hidden agendas, to which Rediger raises his warning. He is concerned that many religious leaders deny the reality of evil and remain ignorant of evil's tactics. The potential damage evil inflicts is his deep concern. It is a kind of spiritual conflict few pastors or laity are equipped to win. Part of the reason may lie in the denial of the reality of evil, the power of evil, and the potential for its influence in every form of human behavior. Evil is present. Evil is a formidable energy.

Is there a defense? The answer is "yes." But evil cannot be faced alone. The first step is prayer, which begins in confession, is petition focused, and is systematic in its approach. A joint management of leadership exercising God's power in Christ's name is essential.

People motivated by evil are real. I faced evil in the church earlier in my career, but I did not name it as such. It wasn't until I began to work in deeply conflicted churches that I began to observe evil at work and identify the fingerprints. The extreme power of evil in human and organized systems became clear. Exorcising evil in our modern religious and political systems is not as simple as naming the evil, casting out the evil, and replacing evil with God's presence as outlined in Mark 5:1–20. Pastors and laity frequently lack the perception and training to fully engage in the struggles they may face. Rediger provides hints along the path to recovery. His signposts include: diligent prayer, renewed energy and commitment in support of the ministry leaders, and community support in a trusted lay leadership focused on their respective missions.

Chapter 11

Morten T. Kelsey

Morten Kelsey, author of *Can Christians Be Educated?* is one of the most prolific and eclectic pastoral writers of his generation. There are few who have so openly attempted to understand pastoral ministry and the relationship between the conscious and the unconscious as it relates to religious practices and healing. He began as an Episcopal priest in a parish in Southern California. His search for truth for his parish, as well as his own internal life, led him to follow the path of analysis and a study of Carl Jung. The search for truth also led him to research and write on the subjects of meditation, dreams, the art of caring, psychology, the charismatic experience, and parapsychology. Although it is always difficult to categorize a writer's contribution to the discussion of ministry, Kelsey is without peer in his attempt to "re-mythologize" Jesus' message, outlook, and proclamations. His search prompted a radical rethinking of New Testament mythology or storytelling.

He sought to understand human beings. His approach to ministry was to uncover man's search for purpose, with the goal of promoting increased mental and physical health. He was a priest, teacher, writer, and pastoral counselor. He was rooted in the church, freed from a worldview that truncates the gospel, and enabled to re-think the church's mission in terms of depth psychology, which addresses the subconscious with its underlying motivations and patterns and the connection to spirit. He wrote thirty-one volumes that touch upon the re-thinking. In one volume, he asks, "Can Christians be educated?" His answer is "yes," provided that Christians can accept a worldview that relates to the life and the teachings of Jesus and the realities of daily events, particularly in terms of mental illness, poverty, and crime. Religious experience, to be vital today, must be informed by intuition, imagination, and dream analysis as doorways to the spiritual life (p. 130).

Kelsey was convinced that the present worldview, which is expressed in most psychologies and most present-day theological discussions, is flawed. The error has been in the failure to take seriously the phenomenon of the supernatural, the mystical experience, and the spiritual potential for healing. "The struggle between good and evil, esthetic utterances, visions and dreams are examples of the reality of a psychic world," he argues (p. 140).

Kelsey bases his authority on not only his parish experiences but also on depth psychology and pastoral counseling. His focus begins with a re-thinking of the mystical as it communicates through the unconscious in its use of symbols, myth (storytelling), and what Jung calls the "collective unconscious." Both Kelsey and Jung conclude that there are two phenomenal worlds and their experiences can be verified. There is the objective physical reality perceived by the five senses. And there is also the psychic world of the unconscious. Examples of the latter's verification are the religious experience and the experiences of dreams, intuition, and healing.

Although both Jung and Kelsey identify an element of dark shadows in the unconscious, representing a struggle between good and evil within a person, the vehicle of the unconscious seems to be directed to help each person follow his or her own personal story. It is this story that relates to the divine and man's surrender to the divine. Theologians would call it the world of the spirit, the religious experience, or the search for the divine. It may represent the theological paradigm shift that is so needed within the Christian faith. Kelsey's findings point to what he calls the psychic language.

The language takes the form of symbols, images, and storytelling. Rembrandt's portrayal of the biblical parable of the Prodigal Son is a vivid example. If it is projected on a screen during morning worship to help people visualize Jesus' message, the audience not only hears but also sees Jesus' parable, almost as if both the sensory world and the spiritual world come together in a doorway between the two worlds.

Extra-sensory perception and telepathic experiences are further examples of the psychic language (p. 31–32). Once acknowledged, these experiences remind the listener of a forgotten language—the language of myth, which is unlimited by time and space that lifts the mind to hear the psychic message. For example, the assassination of Abraham Lincoln on Good Friday, 1864, marks a historical event—the death of Lincoln—while echoing back to the great emancipation of the soul—the crucifixion of Jesus. Thus, this synchronicity, or sign, connects the two events, proclaiming that all men are created equal, all are children of God.

In *Discernment: A Study in Ecstasy and Evil,* Kelsey explains that the myth becomes a reality that is expressed by both imagination and history (p. 95). In terms of the Christian message, Kelsey uses myth to describe the nature of reality. He writes:

> I believe that this basic Christian story is the nearest approxima-
> tion to the nature of ultimate reality that we have. It states that
> the center of reality is love, a loving being, who wishes to relate
> to us and not absorb us into himself or into his infinite mind.
> Something in that universe rebelled and broke away from his
> love and tried to drag the human race into rebellion. It can be
> defeated and has been defeated by the death and resurrection of
> Jesus Christ. As we stay in close relationship with the risen and
> victorious Christ who is essentially related to the source and
> center of love, we can survive and come to wholeness. (p. 96)

From the subject of myth, Kelsey turns his thoughts to the reality of evil and the need to understand darkness and shadows of darkness within each person and the darkness that invades our world. He realizes that once identified, evil cannot be controlled or defeated; nonetheless, he suggests nine concepts to assist in the identifications (*Discernment*, p. 100–105).

First, evil is real and cannot be ignored. The reality must be faced and acknowledged; otherwise, the force of evil, like repressed sin, moves out of the conscious awareness into the unconscious to wreak its painful bondage upon the soul or psyche. To face evil is dangerous, and once it is identified, the threat cannot be minimized. Only Christ's Spirit can face and confront its power within an individual's life.

It is also Kelsey's and Jung's observation that everyone faces the Abyss in some form or at some point in life. "It is better to fall into the pit face first than backwards!" they both agree (p. 101).

Second, to discern evil, one must have an attitude of confession, a sense of personal mistakes, faults, and sins, and a willingness to share these sins with a confessor. Confession may well be the chief defense against the dark force. The relationship between the confession and the confessor may be the bridge to the divine and the source of energy best equipped to confront evil.

Third, the basic myth that evil resides in some physical form and in physical sexuality needs to be re-thought. Gnostic thinking expressed too much of our puritanical theology and has had too much influence on modern Christianity, both Catholic and Protestant. Theology needs radical revision here (*Discernment*, p. 100–105). The revision begins in the acceptance of our physical nature and needs, including sexuality, as good. It is essential that our basic myth be revised from a rejection of sexuality and humanness to one of appreciation for creation.

Fourth, one must pay constant attention to one's outer and inner life. What one does is the best indicator of what one believes and thinks. Evil too often impacts what we do. The best aid for the unconscious and conscious phenomena is the journal practiced with discipline. Listening to dreams, life stories, and indicators to move and act reminds us of the need to integrate both worlds.

I find that time spent in quiet with pen and paper is essential. In the early morning hours, shadow-thoughts may be captured and identified. They speak in symbols and stories that almost always give insights. The knowledge offered might be helpful; it may warn or present hope.

Fifth, discernment of evil and good requires an attitude of compassion and one of non-judgment. Condemnation, too frequently, is self-inflicted and distorts the task of restoration from the wrong things and lesser faults.

Sixth, naked evil seldom can be faced and dealt with without imagination. Rituals and the use of imagination strangely have power that are drawn from the unconscious and equip a person to face evil.

Seventh, to face evil requires courage and a willingness to struggle with darkness. A living faith requires intelligent sacrifice often expressed in self-surrender. The test and trial, not unlike Jesus' wilderness temptation or Elijah's journey in the desert, are illustrative of the cost required (Luke 4:1–13; 1 Kings 19:4–8).

Eighth, in facing evil, one suffers! You will know evil through feelings and sacrifice. "Dark nights of the soul" may invade the journey and must be acknowledged. The figure of the cross takes on a deeper meaning, but not in pietistic forms. It is more like a journey of mortality, facing the hazards that threaten well-being and discipleship.

Ninth, to face evil is a dialectic process, moving from victory to defeat, from some kind of mythological hero to a figure of evil in mythological form. Even though every hero who continues will find places of rest, the process is always dynamic and continues to occur again and again. The basic human problem is the struggle with evil; nonetheless, with imagination and myth, it can be faced (*Discernment,* p. 105).

Evil is not readily understood in most Christian communities, nor is it perceived in community systems or in people until it is too late. When identified, it is often ignored at great cost. Too often, it is perceived as personality dysfunction or a community malady that comes from its culture or injustice suffered. Thus, evil is misunderstood and ultimately ignored. The reason may lie in the attempt to rationalize the causes as faults, mistakes, and oversights rather than sin and the intent to hurt or control.

M. Scott Peck, mentioned earlier, describes the phenomenon of evil in his book *People of the Lie*. He recalls the My Lai Atrocities. On March 16, 1968, American soldiers systematically killed between five to six hundred unarmed women and children in the village of My Lai in South Vietnam (p. 213). Such extreme examples are not as infrequent as we think. Whole cities, countries, and entire cultures have suffered from such unthinkable atrocities. It is a shock when such inhumanity occurs, but it is particularly disturbing when the acts are attributed to the American nation, whose government prides itself on justice and compassion.

Church leaders are too willing to describe conflict within the church's walls in psychological terms: scapegoat, transference, personality dysfunction, cultural disenfranchisement, or simply "incompetent leadership." However, one wonders if evil is not the motivator of the dysfunction and our failure as ministers of Christ to be "stewards of the mysteries of God" (1 Cor. 4:1).

Chapter 12

Henri J. Nouwen

To be a pastor, poet, priest, and shepherd is to be humbled by the tasks faced. Naiveté helps at first. We don't know any better. Later, we recognize the complexities of the issues and the ferocity of what is expected. We are humbled by our mistakes and the failures of our best efforts. To think otherwise is to be infected by the illness of acedia. Acedia is described by the attitude of selfishness; it can be represented by alienation and arrogance. Theologically, it has the face of estrangement, sin, and mental illness. However one describes acedia, it is a kind of darkness clothed in forms few understand except to call it *evil*.

Ministerial work requires all the training and awareness possible. Evil is real. It is powerful. It gives no quarter. One is reminded of John LeCarre's book *Tinker, Tailor, Soldier, Spy*. Agent George Smiley is given the task to root out a mole (double agent) in the British Secret Intelligence Service. You have to be a little of everything to do God's work (a modern George Smiley). You have to be a pastor with heart, a poet of intuition and imagination, a priest of mysteries, and a shepherd who faces his own sins and faults. The ultimate task is to follow in the footsteps of God's Son, to feed and assist the "children of light" to find their way, and to identify "the mole of evil" in people and systems of the church. It is an impossible task aside from God's grace.

Henri Nouwen, an author, priest, and teacher, might not think of himself as a George Smiley, but I find the analogy meaningful as I deal with the complexities of pastoral ministries and marvel at the grace given me. In *The Only Necessary Thing*, Nouwen suggests that evil expresses itself in betrayal, in violence, in hatred, and in suspicion. Evil, in Nouwen's mind, is the absence of God's love. He does not perceive evil as having any alternative but instead as a force in opposition to love. To think otherwise is to exist in illusion, and ultimately, the existence becomes lethal (p. 68–69).

With that understood, man becomes the center of a cosmic battle between God and evil. Evil is the enemy. The individual, the society, the church, and the nation are the battlefields. The clamor of voices is always a part of the battle. The ministry of Jesus and his church are engaged in the struggle. The success of ministry is dependent upon inward and outward journeys. The inward focus is dependent upon reclusion and solitude, with the goal being to face ourselves and to experience the love of the creator.

Nouwen's greatest contribution may well be the process of integrating the feelings of the wounded heart with the connection to the source of healing exemplified in the Trinity—loving Spirit, compassionate Father, and friend in Jesus. From this inward journey, one is equipped for the outer journey, whether working for justice or promoting peacemaking. Right action is a response based upon the voice of intuitive truth, a reaction inspired by the inward journey.

Nouwen recognizes the outer noises as the heartaches of society that often draw out the inner voice of God, much like the thunder, the lightning, and the earthquakes of Elijah's theophany. Only in the inward journey of solitude and reclusion, however, is it possible to hear the "still small voice of God" in the same theophany. It is here also that the battle continues with the voice of evil that whispers the great lie, "God is not with you" (p. 86). Here lies also the great danger for man to be separated from the voice of God and his Son. To be separate, to be exclusive and to exclude, whether Catholic or Protestant, may be man's greatest pitfall and the place where "evil" manifests itself in families and systems.

For example, the tribalism in Africa may well support the evil that affects their society. Genocide and famine characterize so much of this continent that compassion is lost in a black hole of indifference.

Nouwen describes our society as a place of human verbosity and fragmentation. It is a society bombarded by a myriad of images and sounds in all sorts of sizes, colors, and effects (p. 99). The images say, "Eat me, look at me, buy me, hire me, touch me, sleep with me!" The result is a kind of materialism centered in "me," in the "me world," and in like-minded "me people." He calls this the *upward-mobility* that leads to dollars, friendship, popularity, and career progress. It is in direct opposition to the *downward mobility* of Jesus' words, "What have you done to the least of mine, the poor, the refugees, the hungry, crucified humanity?" (Matt. 25:31–46). In these words, Nouwen sees the ground of cosmic battle between good and evil, between God and evil, between Jesus and evil, and between the Spirit and evil.

Nouwen argues the case, pulling theology away from its intellectual practices into the task of ministering to humanity—its wounds and its sins. Nouwen writes:

> We feel like wandering strangers in a fast changing world. But we do not want to escape this world. Instead, we want to be fully part of it without drowning in its stormy waters. We want to be alert and receptive to all that happens around us without being paralyzed by inner fragmentation. We want to travel with open eyes through the valley of tears without losing contact with the one who calls us to a new land … It is indeed like a murmuring stream that continues underneath the many waves of every day and opens the possibility of living in a world without being of it and of reaching out to our God from the center of solitude. (p. 119)

Listen to the words of Brian D. McLaren, in the forward to Frederick Buechner's book *Secrets in the Dark*, as he described his affinity with a new generation of clergy, whose concerns are with light as it confronts shadows. "These young clergy," he writes, "are tired to death of easy answers, and simple steps and cozy scenes with serene porch lights and perfect picket fences. They do not live in that world. They live in a world of thick glasses, gun racks, acne and cancer. And so do the people they preach to" (p. xi).

I too am troubled by the darkness; yet I believe that beyond the darkness is a river of light rippling with life and energy. Set against the darkness, this light beckons! The light is a pervasive, eternal, unquenchable reality in the midst of darkness. Once the light is encountered, however faint, the thirst is quenched, the hunger deepened, and the quest to follow and to fulfill one's destiny is on! It is the task of pastors, poets, priests, and shepherds to witness the light and to draw others to its flame. St. Paul understood the darkness and the shadows. Yet, upon encountering the light, he was forever changed. He spent his life pointing out the eternal light, which still burns for us today. Listen to Paul's words of encouragement from 2 Corinthians 4:7–12, translated into contemporary language in *The Message* by Eugene H. Peterson:

> If you look at us, you might well miss the brightness. We carry this precious Message around in unadorned clay pots of our ordinary lives. That's to prevent anyone from confusing God's incomparable power with us. As it is, there's not much chance of that. You know for yourselves that we're not much to look at. We've been surrounded and battered by troubles, but we're not demoralized; we're not sure what to do, but we know that God knows what to do; we've been spiritually terrorized, but God hasn't left our side; we've been thrown down, but we haven't broken. What they did to Jesus, they do to us—trial and torture, mockery and murder; what Jesus did among them, he does in us—he lives! So we're not giving up. How could we? Even though on the outside it often looks like things are falling apart on us, on the inside where God is making new life, not a day goes by without his unfolding grace. (p. 2099)

Part 4

Paradigm Shift

Reflections on Parish Worship

Any discussion of a parish in worship begins with the community and the pastor of that community. To the degree in which they honor, love, and give themselves to the worship of God lies the value of their joint efforts. As I reflect on my work as a parish minister, I know the complexities of which I speak and am humbled by the task of sharing my insights with you, the reader.

Renowned theologian Joseph A. Sittler, in his book *Grace Notes and Other Fragments*, described the pastor as the object of maceration, as being chopped up into small pieces (p. 57–58). It is the burden that the pastor's time, perceived sense of vocation, vision of his or her central task, and mental life are often cluttered with a roll of blueprints, the bank statement, the mission board requests, and samples of asphalt tile for a leaky roof. The stress, the demands, and the long hours are perhaps the most difficult of professional disciplines and callings within our society.

The pastor must throw caution out the window to maintain his own integrity as God's man, as pastor and fellow worshipper, while refusing to be pulled apart. "He has to dance and live his faith as a ragged garment, often with seams showing and tears open to the winds," Frederic Buechner notes in *Listening to Your Life* (p. 34).

The pastor's central focus is the worship of God and leadership of worship. He does both with tears and laughter, imagination and drama. It takes a lifetime to master the craft. He learns to pray, to listen, and to feel the depth and crisis of the parish and God's process in all the human tragedies and joys within the parish and the society in which he lives.

The parish lives within culture; it cannot escape the culture. It is in this sense that the pastor must face the tensions of faith and the tragedies of the daily news with its crimes and wars and attempt to preach and live out his message without intellectualization or evasion. He is called to lead the worship of God. He is also called to do so by God, if he has read Isaiah (6:1–13) and finds application. If he does, the pastor senses his call and God's response of encouragement. If he (or she) doesn't heed the call and listen to God's word to him, he fails himself and the God who has called him.

Thus, the focus of any valued reflection upon worship and man's attitude toward the worship of God begins here. The words of James Muilenburg, an Old Testament teacher with few equals, seem fitting for the beginning of the context of worship reflection. Muilenburg wrote in *The Way of Israel*:

The sense of obligation lies deep in the heart of every man sometimes obscurely, sometimes distraughtly or oppressively, but to some degree or another, however, variously conceived or deeply felt, it belongs to the fabric of his consciousness. Whenever he is disposed to be reflective or thoughtful concerning himself, he is aware that he has done those things which he ought not to have done and has left undone those things which he ought to have done. "What ought I to do?" belongs to the native speech of men. Not Eve alone or Cain alone hears the voice, "What have you done?" All of us have listened to those words, and have been confused or embarrassed or stricken by them. What is it, then, that is required of us? Israel's way is to change our neutral and impersonal passives into the personal ultimate active: "What does the Lord require? What is his will and purpose for me?" To these questions the whole Old Testament, from first page to last, gives its urgent and impassive reply. For turn where we will—to the earliest legends and traditions of the patriarchs; to the teachings of the leaders (whether parent, judge, king, or priest); to the narratives of the historians; to the calls, oracles, and visions of the prophets sent from God; to the hymns, prayers, and thanksgivings of the cultic ministrants; to the counsels and directions of the wise—everywhere we encounter in one form or another, the category "thou shall" and "thou shall not." Everywhere Israel is summoned to hearing: "Hear, O Israel!" The imperative and the vocative belong together, for words are being spoken to which man must give heed and they are words addressed to him. (p. 63)

The influence of Reinhold Niebuhr upon worship context should also be remembered. As one of America's most influential Christian scholars and pastors, he too has few equals. Niebuhr wrote in *Justice and Mercy* of his concern that preachers show excellence in their craft as proclaimers and that they relate to individuals—both male and female—as they live out their faith and make applications to the social dimensions in society.

In an address to one entering class of students at Union Theological Seminary, he described the Protestant church as too dependent on preaching. That is to say, "The main virtue of the liturgical church is that it isn't so dependent upon the sermon. If a sermon is bad, you can still stand it, because you have the whole drama of faith portrayed in the liturgy" (p. 1).

Niebuhr expressed concern that worship should demonstrate not only the law of love and compassion as its crown but also that its servant, the law of justice, should be equally exercised. He recalled the words of the prophet Amos, who was, as were many of the prophets, critical of all religions that were not creative in seeking a policy of social justice, and quoted him to make his point: "I hate, I despise your feasts, and I take no delight in solemn assemblies … but let justice roll down like water, and righteousness like an overflowing stream" (Amos 6:16).

Reinhold Niebuhr suggests that the pastor or priest can be the mediator of God's judgment and also his mercy. He felt that the problem of worship lay at the feet of the proclaimers. He suggests that too often the preacher lacked charity and humility. Nevertheless, he wrote, "The older I grow in the ministry, the more I am impressed by good pastors, who work with those who must be broken before they can be rebuilt; and those who are broken and must be rebuilt … In all the pastoral duties, a compassionate heart will show forth in the spirit of Christ, and save the church from triviality" (p. 9).

From those facets of worship, the failures and the gifts, we find ourselves in modern time polarized over culture. All three scholars, Sittler, Muilenburg, and Reinhold Niebuhr, provide a common focus upon the church's efforts to worship God in God's holy community, while engaging culture with some sense of balance. The options to ignore culture, withdraw from culture, or to embrace culture, in my opinion, all result in a dysfunctional church. It is the difficult task, to use Muilenburg's terms, of following the imperative and the vocation together. For Jesus proclaimed, "You shall love the Lord, your God with all your heart, and with all your soul, and with all your strength, and with all your mind, and your neighbor as yourself" (Luke 9:25–27).

It is clear to me that the Christian church has the responsibility and the capability to integrate the *vocative* and the *imperative*. The Parable of the Good Samaritan is an example. The love of God and the love of neighbor come together in the mercy expressed.

Jesus expected his church to do the same. It is my observation that whenever justice is taken out of worship, Christ's church fails God's imperative and the vocative is broken.

In summary, the negative contribution or impact of the Christian church stems directly from the failure to confront culture and demand justice within culture as Jesus modeled it. In fact, Jesus' death and his resurrection are the "Christus Victus" over culture and ultimately the evil that motivates injustice and chaos. Despite the teachings of Jesus and the church's proclamation, the problem endures.

The fact that injustice and chaos have been a part of the church's history is reflected in its present conflict and divisiveness. The issue of *culture and gospel* was not always clearly stated nor accepted by the church until the Reformation. The aftermath of two world wars, the destruction of half of Europe, and the passivity of the German church during the genocide of the Jewish community may well have awakened the American church; however, the present conflict of modern worship practices confirms that the problem persists to this day.

H. Richard Niebuhr, in *Christ and Culture*, focused the church's attention upon these issues some sixty-plus years ago. He based his work on Ernst Trosltsch's book *The Social Teaching of the Christian Churches* (p. xii). I believe there has been no equal to Niebuhr's analysis to this day, in spite of the fact that it is frequently overlooked. He proposed that there were five perspectives in the debate over the problems of Christ and culture. Briefly stated, they are: "Christ against culture; the Christ of culture; Christ above culture; Christ and culture in paradox; and Christ the transformer of culture" (pp. 40–45).

It is classic H. Richard Niebuhr that suggests that every Christian generation has dealt with the vitality of its faith and its responsibility to culture or to its society. He reminds the church of God's judgment on Israel, precisely because it failed to responsively govern its society with justice for the needy, the poor, the widow, the orphan, and the imprisoned. He based his call to the church upon Isaiah 10. This was the first part of the context as he defined it. The second part of the context was St. Paul's description of the living community called the church—its spirit, its gifts, its energy, or its compassion—taken from 1 Corinthians 12 and Augustine's *City of God* (p. xii).

The five sides of the debate proposed by Niebuhr represented the typical answers to the enduring problems of Christ and culture and, ultimately, the basis of the present conflict about worship. It is fair, he argues, to suggest Christ is found in all five sides of the debate; this does not make the definition of Christ or culture easy. For Niebuhr, the problem of Christianity and civilization lies in authority. Is one loyal to the church or is one loyal to the state? To put it another way, the tension between Christ and culture is the cross.

There was also the tension of defining culture and Christianity. For example, what does it mean to be a follower of Jesus Christ? What does it mean to believe in Jesus Christ? What does it mean to define culture? Niebuhr suggests at least three descriptions for Jesus Christ and realizes the descriptions are merely a movement toward definition. The suggested descriptions are as follows: 1) the teacher and new law giver; 2) the revealer of incarnate truths and the new life man encounters; and 3) the new community of the Holy Catholic Church, developing a new society that cures by the love of God in word and sacrament (p. 12). He recognized the complexity of the views, but, nevertheless, he moved the discussion toward an understanding of Jesus Christ by description rather than definition:

> The power and attraction Jesus Christ exercises over men never comes from him alone, but from him as Son of the Father. It comes from him in his *sonship* in a double way, as man living to God and God living with men. Belief in him and loyalty to his cause involves man in the double movement from world to God and from God to world. Even when theologians fail to do justice to this fact, Christians living with Christ in their cultures are aware of it. For they are forever being challenged to abandon all things for the sake of God; and forever being sent back into the world to teach and practice all things that have been commanded them. (p. 29, emphasis added)

Niebuhr then gives his attention to culture as it is connected to whatever particular civilization that Christianity is intertwined with and a member of. He suggests that culture is the total process of human activity. The result of such activity is found in common speech (p. 32–34).

But there is also more. Culture comprises language, habits, ideas, beliefs, customs, social organization, inherited artifacts, technical processes, and values. This is "the world" described by the New Testament writers. Culture then becomes the social heritage one receives and transmits. Cultural achievement are the values realized in temporal and material goods (p. 36–38). It is the conservation of such values. It is finally the pluralism manifold in society's weaving interest. There are, of course, predominate forces within every culture that the Christian movement lives with that require an ability to cope and adapt within or lose the balance that is necessary to live in two worlds—one of worship and service and the other the civilization in which Christianity dwells. Thus, Neibuhr's analysis of the five positions of the tensions between faith and culture may be restated with greater depth.

The first position is Christ against culture. This position stands against culture and the authority of the society that promotes the culture and defends it. The challenge is an either/or proposition. Follow Christ in his opposition to culture and its values or reject Christianity and embrace culture. To be a Christian from this position is to withdraw from culture (the world) and separate oneself from the society. It is literally to be separate from society. It is often represented by missionaries who require their converts to renounce their customs and institutions (p. 40–41).

The second position seeks to embrace culture and solve the dilemma between Christianity and culture by suggesting an agreement between Christ and civilization. Jesus becomes the hero of human culture, and Christ represents man's greatest human achievement. He is the combination of human values. To Christians with such a view, there is a close relationship between Christianity and western civilization (p. 44).

The third position between cultures and the church seeks either to combine or unify the polarization. Thus, Christ becomes above culture and becomes the new value carrier, or Christ becomes a part of culture but also above culture. It is a type of synthetic that interconnects and is represented in early and modern times (p. 42).

The fourth position is Christ and culture in a paradox. Duality and authority are recognized, and Christ and culture are accepted. The tension between them is acknowledged; yet Christ requires Christianity to be in obedience to the culture. Martin Luther represented this position, and the danger of this view was represented by the passivity of the German church during World War II. There were a few exceptions, such as the Theological Declaration of Barmen, debated and adopted by the German Evangelical Church at the first Confessional Synod in May of 1934. The chief item of discussion was an appeal to stand firm against the German Christian accommondation to national socialism and the Nazi party.

The fifth position is what Niebuhr calls the "transformer of culture." This position suggests Christ is opposed to all human instructions and customs and calls the church not to separate, or endure, but to convert man, his society, and his culture. Augustine and John Calvin represented such thought, and these ideas have continued to this day with such writers as Dietrich Bonhoeffer (p. 43).

With such a discussion, one is led to return to the biblical context of Christ and culture—i.e., to live in the world and not be a part of it. Consider first Jesus' dialogue with Pilate. Jesus said to Pilate, "My kingdom is not of this world. If my kingdom were of this world, my followers would be fighting to keep me from being handed over to the Jews" (John 18:36). The implication is that Jesus ignored culture and in doing so refused to reform the Judaism of his day—i.e., he came into the world to abolish culture that was bound up with religion and tradition.

The second context for biblical thought is found in St. Paul's letter to the Roman Christians. St. Paul writes, "Do not be conformed to this world [age], but be transformed by the renewing of your mind, so that you may discern what is the will of God—what is good and acceptable, and [what is] perfect" (Rom. 12:2).

The transformation St. Paul speaks about is a *mystical metamorphism* enabled by a faith in Jesus Christ. The age or world to come has already begun. So though we are in this world, we are compelled to live for God but not to be conformed to any other standard except Christ's kingdom (Fitzmyer, p. 641).

The metamorphosis changes the believers' way of thinking, as well as the way of willing and doing (behavior). It is a renewal of the mind. The metamorphism is inward, not external. It is the seal of the intellect and morality. The metamorphism is brought about by the indwelling of God's Spirit through faith and baptism. The results are *the children of God.*

Paul sums up what living by faith in Jesus Christ is and what becoming children of the light means. St. Paul was dealing with the harmony of the community living in a new age called to overcome evil with good. Thus, Romans 12:2 may be the most profound passage of the New Testament!

In Jesus' and St. Paul's minds, the Spirit was the means to discern how to live *in* this world and not be *of* the world. The children of God were to live by the inner will of God in the metamorphism, by the good recognized in the metamorphism, and by the conduct guided by the metamorphism. Culture was to be subordinated in every way. Culture was *not* to be ignored, but rather it was to be engaged as a struggle with principalities (Rom. 8:38).

It must be noted that St. Paul also personally struggled with the mystical metamorphism and his culture. His debate with Peter at Antioch over the Jewish Christians' demand for Gentile Christians to be circumcised is a good example of religious culture's impact on the new church (Fitzmyer, p. 638, 640–641). Paul was concerned that Jewish culture would rob the non-Jewish converts of religious identity and integrity. His focus was upon the age of the present and its transformation into the coming world. It was a call to nonconformity and a concern for a transformed culture. His focus was the corrupted state of the society, its mixture of good and evil, too close together to identify—only to be transformed to a new heaven and a new earth.

So we are *not* to be conformed to culture. Perhaps this is why Jesus said, "I have come to set a man against his father, and a daughter against her mother and a daughter-in-law against her mother-in-law, and a man's foes will be those of his own household. He who loves father or mother more than me is not worthy of me; and he who loves son or daughter more than me is not worthy of me" (Mark 10:35–37 RSV).

Paul Tillich, in his sermon *Do Not Be Conformed*, described what this kind of non-conformity ultimately is: "It is to protest idolatry in ourselves; it is to protest the idolatry in our world and in our church" (p. 84).

Henri Nouwen, in *The Only Necessary Thing*, gave us a poetic description of the modern man's struggle with the biblical context of living *in* the world and not being *of* the world:

> More than ever we feel like wandering strangers
> In a fast-changing world
> But we do not want to escape this world.
> Instead we want to be fully part of it
> We want to be alert and receptive to all
> That happens around us without being
> Paralyzed by inner fragmentation.
> We want to travel with open eyes through
> The valley of tears without losing contact
> With the one who call us to a new land.
> We want to respond with compassion to all those
> Whom we meet on our way and ask for
> A hospitable place to stay while
> Remaining solidly rooted in the
> Intimate love of God.
> The prayer of the heart shows us one possible way.
> It is indeed like a murmuring stream
> That continues underneath the many
> Waves of everyday life
> And opens the possibility of living
> In the world, without being of it
> And of reaching out to our God from
> The center of our solitude. (p. 119)

Culture and Worship Today

William D. Dyrness, in *A Primer on Christian Worship,* identifies the tragic polarization of the idea of culture adoption and the confrontation of culture. He poses the question, "Where is the problem of Christ and culture today?" (p. 146).

The discussion is in a theological and liturgical quagmire, without a visible pathway to connect the variable opinions and movements within the Christian communities. The forces, instead of bridging the church differences, seem determined to pull the community apart without a realization of the dangers or the consequences (p. 147). Those, for example, who stress the need for content in liturgy and its historical development—the sacred traditions, its music, its words—find little need to engage contemporary seekers, while those interested in a direct connection with culture find no interest in historical liturgy or the foundations of the church. They are totally at odds with each other and refuse to listen to the concerns of those who oppose them.

The cultural revolution exemplified by the "Next Church Movement" is another example of this polarization, explains Frank Burch Brown in *Inclusive Yet Discerning.* "The revolution has arrived," the leaders of this movement state. "Embrace the culture!" The motive is to bring more contemporary forms of worship and a more seeker-comfortable community into existence. It is called "modern evangelism." But the change comes at a great cost. Such embracing ignores the value of imagery, symbols, authority, and identity. Biblical connections are severed. The vision is, "No to spires, crosses, robes, clerical collars, pews, kneelers, biblical gobbledygook, and thoughtful prayer. No calls to justice! No calls to responsibility! No pipe organs! No hymns! No dress up, but dress down! No collection plates either!" How the bills get paid is never mentioned (p. xiii).

In short, worship is eclectic. Theology is flexible. Age and color diversity are ignored. Culture is embraced. Theology and biblical foundation are sacrificed. This approach is dangerous because the church is then faced by a culture that is almost entirely visually mediated. The movement thus engages its culture with a gospel of "Happy Times," and it walks hand in hand *without* a sense of justice. It is an unfortunate diversion of Jesus' gospel and falsifies the witness of the church. The church needs to adapt, but not at the sacrifice of its message.

One must also note that the recent analysis of cultural trends indicates that sixty percent of the emerging populations are visual learners. To engage the present generation in worship, music, drama, and art is essential, explains Dryness (p. 147).

The church does require more and more eclectic approaches. However, what is at stake at the deepest level is a serious distortion of Jesus' message, particularly when he confronts culture. The search for justice and holiness are valued issues not to be compromised, as John D. Witvliet notes in Charles E. Farhadion's book *Christian Worship World Wide.* We need to be reminded of Jesus, who faced the issue of temple power, challenged the established leadership of Jewish religion, and engaged actively in the struggle between culture and gospel. Money changers in the place of prayer crossed the boundaries for Jesus. His call to reestablish a theology of compassion, justice, humility, and a concern for the weak, poor, and disabled was balanced against the demands of culture. What were and still are at stake include the church's identity, authority, and integrity. Jesus' message, preached and lived with his mindset, engages the sufferings in society and in communities. Many "lighthouse communities," however, ignore the poverty of the inner city, race conflicts, and even national disasters, bringing only sadness to those seeking to balance culture and faith.

Dennis T. Olsen, in *Touching the Altar of God,* reminds the church of its detractors and its need to speak helpfully and powerfully to the culture. He also calls the church to its biblical foundations and its integrity:

We live in the midst of worship wars, terrorist war battles of denominational unrest, the disestablishment of the church, increasing blindness toward the needs of the poor, human ravaging of the world's environment and all manners of personal and community unrest and turmoil. (p. 30)

Every generation wrestles with questions of integrity as the good news of the gospel is translated into fresh cultural idioms. However, it is my observation that too much of the church is preoccupied with its own survival and too readily withdraws to its catacomb of community support. As Cornelius Plantinga, Jr., and Sue Rozeboom, in *Discerning the Spirits*, remind us:

> But here lies a famous problem. If Christians fail to engage the world of secular culture in order to protect them from its temptations, they cannot live and witness in the real world. They can't even understand it. They can't address unbelievers in language unbelievers understand. But if Christians get close enough to secular culture to understand it, to witness to it, to try in some ways to reform it or even to use it in the worship of God—how will Christians keep from being seduced by the worldliness within this culture, and how will they keep from their worship of God? It is a strange paradox and a difficult maze for God's people to navigate. (p. 84)

Contemporary theologian Matthew M. Boulton in *God Against Religion* helped us to re-think worship through the minds of Karl Barth and Martin Luther. Boulton echoes the words of the prophets who suggest a presumptuous spirit, cynicism, and sentimentality are not justifications for God's favor. His thesis is twofold: one is that God is against religion and pre-eminently against worship in religion; and secondly, in Jesus Christ, God transforms worship from an event of fatal separation into an event of saving reconciliation. In other words, in Jesus Christ, God undertakes and overcomes worship's disastrous drama and transforms the liturgy into efforts to worship; it is a form of grace that enables the best of efforts and the poorest examples to enter into renovation and vicarious participation of God with his people. I see it as a valid dance that requires a deep appreciation of grace and humanity. To use Boulton's metaphor, "The religious sword is conquered, to be sure, but not destroyed; the blade is preserved and remade into a plowshare" (p. 6).

From the best reflections on religious struggles, one is drawn back to St. Paul's letters to the Corinthian church. Paul's deeply felt idea of one body with many members is essential. His poem of a more excellent way, the way of love, lifts the mind and heart to the deepest source of service. Love is the ground and purpose of the church's ministry, despite the pulling apart by evangelical, Pentecostal forces and reformed, liturgical movements today. The church is in crisis, caught in an either/or mindset. Either the church engages culture or embraces culture with Jesus' gospel. To withdraw from culture seems to be a pathway to defeat.

The ultimate tragedy may lie in God's withdrawal. It is to man's peril when faced with enlightenment to reject it. The experience of the holy, insights to truth, and mystical encounters of God touching man are all examples of God reaching out. To ignore such love, unfortunately, results in man's uncertainty and estrangement.

Certainly, there is a continuous need to connect theology and worship. They have for too long walked down opposite sides of the street, too often ignoring each other. There is a need to revisit the connection between liturgy and ministry, especially the ministry to the impoverished. It should be noted that the contemporary church often reflects a dubious ignorance of theology and tradition. Why? Perhaps theology has not been rooted in the daily experience of the worshiping community. Theology, with all its power and substance, must return to the parish in ways that can be understood by the community.

Kathleen Norris, in her article "Sinatra in the Bell Tower," leveled the serious charge that "worship has become light and frivolous instead of being grounded in the biblical" (p. 301). Most of contemporary worship appears to be a litany of repetition to lead God's people into emotional responses without content or thoughtful pointers to mystery. If we are not to conform to this age or world but be transformed as a "metamorphism" through the Spirit of Christ, then the discernment of God's worship must be based upon standards not of the present culture but upon the will of God, the good of God, and the acceptance of God so that the perfect might be lived out in the midst of culture (Rom. 12:1–2). Such is the merit of well thought-out theology, the task of the theologian, and the mission of the parish minister to connect with the church community.

There are some who argue against conformity and unity. They suggest that separate expressions of the Christian faith are necessary and a good thing. However, one wonders if, had the call for unity been heard, the separation of the eastern and western church would have occurred.

Joseph D. Small, Director of Theology Worship and Education Ministries, Presbyterian Church (USA), notes in *Christian Worship in Reform Churches Past and Present*, "The sixteenth century protestant Reformation led to unprecedented fragmentation of the Christian church" (p. 311). Schism was a reality, and it seems to have continued in every century since, which should cause the church to reflect and mend its theological fences.

H. Richard Niebuhr argued this premise as well by saying that denominationalism represents the moral failure of Christianity. The present theological and cultural fragmentation seems to confirm these points. Denomenationalism may well be one of the greatest barriers to evangelism and Jesus' message of love.

Chapter 14

Imagination

I have come to the rather simplistic notion that imagination is
the capacity to image a world beyond what is obviously given.
                                        —Walter Brueggemann

Tourists flock to the Loretto Chapel in Sante Fe, NM, to see this beautiful and miraculous staircase. Touted as an unsolved mystery, legend tells of an unknown carpenter who accomplished this engineering feat in answer to the Sisters of Loretto's prayer petition. Some say it was St. Joseph himself who answered the call.

Imagination in worship and spiritual practices may seem an unlikely prism through which insight and faith may occur. Walter Brueggemann's study of imagination is essential to this discussion. A renowned theologian and author, Brueggemann, like most well-trained scholars and students of the Bible, was trained in historical criticism, which requires interpreting the text in light of the culture and context in which it occurred. The task is to grasp the biblical author's meaning and move beyond it, guarding against simple moralization and the projection of one's personal feelings onto the text.

Through the use of imagination, the modern preacher formulates his greatest contribution and this may represent the most significant paradigm shift from the early church to the present. In fact, all effective preaching makes the analogous bridge from the first century to the present. The path grows unclear at times; yet the road to the kingdom and God's world are deeply needed and sought. People are drawn to worship in order to grasp the bridge. Imagination enables this to happen within the context of quality preaching and the worship of God.

Yet, Brueggemann has much to say on the importance of imagination when interpreting Scripture. He discovered, almost by accident, that if he wanted to be pertinent, compelling, or contemporary, he needed to be alert and receptive to unexpected acts of imagination.

Sparks of imagination ignite when the preacher stretches and pulls the text and its implications beyond the printed words. Energy and excitement are released. The fire of imagination may seem theologically dangerous, but handled with care, the released energy touches the listener at deep, spiritual levels, dislodging old prejudices and preconceived notions and depositing warm ashes of grace. Imagination, Brueggemann discovered, is an avenue to the sacred and sparks a renewed proclamation of the gospel.

In an interview with Bradford Winters of *Image Journal* (#55), Brueggemann had this to say:

> I have come to the rather simplistic notion that imagination is the capacity to image a world beyond what is obviously given. That's the work of poets and novelists and artists—and that's what biblical writers mostly do. I think that's why people show up at church. They want to know whether there is any other world available than the one we see, which we can hardly bear. I have subsumed a lot of those ideas under the rubric of imagination for my own work. (p. 52)

If Walter Brueggemann is correct, the use of imagination may well be the doorway to rethinking the focus of the Christian church. The proclamation of the gospel requires imagination. In fact, it demands it. But the use of imagination is not limited to the pulpit. Imagination must stimulate the prayer life and worship of the Christian community. Church leaders at all levels need to engage and confront culture. The Social Economic Political Power Structure (SEPPS) must be identified and resisted with the power of imagination.

Following are several areas where imagination finds focus.

Dreams

The use of dreams is an untapped source for imagination in the church today. Yet dreams have biblical precedence. Consider Joseph's interpretation of Pharaoh's dream of economic feast and famine in his homeland and Joseph's eventual rise to power in Egypt. Consider also the dream of a New Testament Joseph, revealing God's plan for the birth of Jesus through Mary. Consider St. Peter's dream recorded in Acts 10, in which God confronts the notion of clean and unclean animals, and Cornelius, the centurion, who is led by a dream to seek out Peter. Peter's dream and the centurion's response would change forever the attitude of the Jewish-Christian community toward the Hellenistic world and make Peter's revised message all-inclusive.

I once had a dream that inspired the poem "The Dance." The dancer was close to our family and often did sacred dance in worship. The poem illustrates not only the influence of imagination but also the use of dreams to convey truth.

The Dance

A young woman danced.
Her body slim, graceful, she danced.
Artfully, across the space
The music played,
Only for her did it play.
From the background came the words:
"I knew it! I knew she had it!"
All those days,
Retraced steps,
Faulted starts,
Mistakes made.
I watched excellence
Displayed.
There was beauty there; joy there too.
Laughter and cheer arose
As if I danced the dance and knew
The wonder of her dance.
Who watched off-stage?
He spoke, without doubt,
As he said.
"I knew it. I knew she had it."
Too dark to see his face
This prophet who knew
Her and her grace.
Who is this prophet who taught us to dance
And helps us to teach the dance?
Always in the shadow, but always there.

—Chet B. Gean
from *Thoughts in Time* ©2003

A struggling congregation was building a new church in Omak, Washington. Money was tight. The mason wanted an exorbitant fee for the stone and brick work. Kenneth Dick, a member of the church and a lumber mill worker offered to tackle the job. He had no experience in brick or stone masonry, but the church leaders trusted him. After seven years, the building was completed, including a wall that was fifty feet by nine feet, a retaining wall, and stone steps. The church was pleased, but Kenneth was not satisfied. He asked if he might erect a stone mosaic at the entrance to the church. To his surprise, the leaders agreed.

Now he had to come up with an idea. He prayed for wisdom and guidance. One midnight, he awoke suddenly from a dream. In the dream, he received a postcard on which was a picture of a completed rock mosaic.

"I wonder if I could possibly make a wall like that?" he asked upon awakening. He quickly made a colored sketch of his idea and presented it to the church elders. They liked it.

"Now where will I get the stone to create the colors and textures?" he wondered. "I need brown with the texture of wood." Then he remembered a trip he and his wife had taken up the Twisp River to War Creek in 1940. He had seen the perfect brown rock, but it was now twenty-five years later. "Can I get my truck up that remote fire-trail road?" he wondered. He was able to make the trip and split off enough of that rock to make a large cross.

The central figure in the mosaic required black stone. After much effort, he was ready to give up. Then the Lord directed him to the perfect source, where he was able to gather just enough to do the job. He created the pattern of a man from cardboard and spent two weeks chiseling the stone into shape.

In God's perfect timing, a couple came to the valley to pick apples and showed up for church. Kenneth and his wife invited them home for Sunday dinner. While discussing the project, Kenneth told the couple that he was stumped on how to find green rock needed for the hillside. "There's a quarry in the mountain up by Addy, Washington, near our place. You'll find plenty there."

Today the rock mosaic stands as a testament. The church has twice been destroyed by arson fire; yet the rock wall remains. When viewers gaze at the figure of a man weighed down by the cross, Kenneth hopes they will be reminded of Christ's sacrifice and that they will determine to carry their own crosses faithfully.

Photo Provided by the family of Kenneth Dick

One of my brightest interns experienced an archetypal dream with a particular truth that played out in our lives and in the life of the church community. It shows the power of imagination to guide the church:

Chet and Arline (pastor's wife) have invited Pete and me to visit their church. The church is on a hill, a hill that appears to be in the wilderness to some degree because the hill is completely natural, covered with trees, bushes, and rocks except for the building at the top.

Chet has started a tradition of doing the opening liturgy at the bottom of the hill with the whole church gathered in a small clearing. Then he leads the congregation in climbing up this rocky, narrow, and very steep path up to the church. It has to be climbed single file, with arms outstretched for balance, and hands gripping dirt, rocks, or the strong branches on either side.

The large open space inside the church is dark. There are rows of seats set in a segment of a circle around this space that has a huge, black floor area. Imagine a concert stage that is dimly lit so that you can't quite see where the space ends. Close to the seats on the right side, there is a black piano with various electronic gear set up as if for a rock concert. Way across the space to the left side, there appears to be a large choir and an orchestra.

Chet seems to be preaching, but there is no pulpit. Instead he wanders around in the large space left between the various musicians. He does some interesting body movements as he speaks, like little dance steps and twirls. Then suddenly the church is transformed.

Now it is this beautiful, very traditional church that is all in whites and is sunlit. Chet is standing behind but also at one corner of the communion table. Perhaps it is made out of white marble. It seems to be quite high, and reminds me of the altars where priests elevate the communion symbols. Chet is just finishing up presiding over communion with elders assisting.

Then he begins to preside over this new sacrament that was his brainchild. I see him with a silver or gold chalice containing a lump of molten, translucent red candy. (Imagine Red Jolly Ranchers in a semi-soft stage.) I see him speaking to the congregation as he forms this candy himself into little spirals. This is how he does it: he pinches at the lump, which seems like it must be hot enough to burn his fingers, and pulls out a strand of the still moldable candy which is about an eighth of an inch in diameter. He wraps the strand in a spiral around a wooden stick that is about a quarter inch in diameter. As he wraps, the candy hardens into a hard, translucent spiral, which he then removes from the stick to begin a new piece. He makes each tube about an inch and a quarter in length. Each person in the congregation will get a piece.

The interpretation of dreams requires practice and discipline. It is not to be feared. In fact, the more it is practiced, the stronger the bridge between the two spheres within the brain becomes. New connections link the conscious to the unconscious and one's essential being to the mystical voice of God. Dream interpretation begins with associations, preferably in a group setting, where an attempt is made to interpret symbols, reflect on meanings, and clarify truth that is both personal and contextual.

In the case of the intern's dream, the reader is projected into a dark theater, symbolizing the current bleak financial and spiritual outlook within the parish. When the center stage is filled with instruments, music, dance, and drama, the worshippers are transformed. Entering the mystery, they move from darkness to light. The unorthodox Eucharist sparks the imagination, promoting healing, inspiration, and renewed childlike faith in the abundant grace of God.

I recall as a boy stopping at the corner drug store for a large bag of cinnamon candy before the Saturday afternoon matinee. It was a wonderful delight, chosen for its "hotness." Nothing topped a wild western, popcorn, and cinnamon candy. The worship of God should be just as hot, filled with the drama of life and sparked by God's Spirit.

Visual Art

The visual arts provide a very effective link to imagination. A stroll through a cathedral with its stained-glass windows, frescos, and flickering candles evokes veneration and awe. The American

Catholic Church's portrayal of the stages of the cross invites congregants to ponder the passion of Christ. Early American Protestant churches made use of stained-glass windows to connect worshippers with Christ's ministry and create a space for reflection and connection.

Many modern American churches have abandoned the visual arts all together. The modern start-up church may hold services in a school gymnasium or even a shopping mall. Mega churches,

geared for mass-media presentations, strip the altar of all but the barest necessities to make room for multi-purpose activities, rock bands, and media screenings. Yet even in these stark settings, or perhaps especially in these settings, the visual arts can provide a bridge to the imagination and inspire meaningful worship.

Imagination expressed in the visual arts may enable the parish to grasp more readily the message proclaimed, if used in conjunction with Scripture and proclamation. *The Smithsonian*, January 2009, records that in 1888, Vincent Van Gogh explained, "Imagination ... enables us to create a more exalting and consoling nature than what just a glance of reality ... allows us to perceive. A starry sky, for example, well—it's a thing that I'd like to try to do" (p. 68–73).

Later that year, Van Gogh painted *The Starry Night over Rhone* (Trachtman, p. 68). His imaginative masterpiece bridges the gap between the mystical and material world. The darkness of the sky embraces the chaos and difficulty of life, and the harbor lights and stars signal hope. Thus art and the imagination it inspires readily become vehicles of the unconscious and inroads to the mystical.

A second example of the imaginative use of art concerns Rembrandt's masterpiece *The Return of the Prodigal*, the original of which is now housed in the Hermitage in St. Petersburg, Russia. Henri Nouwen in *The Return of the Prodigal Son: The Story of Homecoming* draws on his study of the painting to enter into the mystery of the prodigal's reconciliation (p. 69).

When the painting is viewed in worship, the Scripture and the spoken message take on a new dimension. Imagination opens the door; figures come to life. The elder brother seems less rigid in Rembrandt's portrayal, giving hope to archetypal sibling jealousies. The beloved father is made more real, searing our imagination with the burden of parenthood. The shoulders of the penitent prodigal are lightened by forgiveness. A close look reveals the painter himself inviting the viewers to enter the scene. Through art-inspired imagination, the mind and heart are stirred. The Spirit moves, and

Jesus, the master storyteller, interacts with today's disciples. The community understands, and I believe God smiles.

Poetry

Through poetry, words and metaphorical images merge, capturing the imagination and joining heart and intellect. Like dreams, the use of poetry also has biblical precedence. Most of the beloved, traditional hymns of the Christian church have their roots in the poetry of Scripture. The lyrics of King David's psalms were lifted directly from biblical text and set to music. In recent history, the psalms also have found their expression in praise songs, which extract key poetic phrases from the text.

From Isaiah comes the poetic vision of the Seraphs, their song, and their music. Here real poetry begins as the poet illustrates the paradox of every pastor who preaches and every listener who has tried to listen. The word must be brought to life through the imagination, and only with an imagination empowered by God's Spirit can one understand the deeper message and make meaningful connections (Isa. 6:11–13).

St. Paul's words, often translated into prose, are another use of imagination in poetry. Clearly his words are a call to ministry but

also to the hidden application of the cross. Read St. Paul's words in 1 Corinthians 1:17–25 arranged in poetic form, and feel the power of his thoughts.

Meditation and Visual Imagery

To image is to meditate—to be still and listen. To know God is to visualize with imagination. The Psalmist pointed to this stillness. "Be still and know that I am God!" (Ps. 46:10). But to remain still, to contemplate and ponder, requires a form or image as a focal point. For the early church, this focus was the Son of Man. He was the image of identification. He was and is Jesus Christ, whose image is captured in laughter as well as in suffering. But only with the use of imagination is the bridge made. Thus, to meditate and to pray requires an image, figure, or symbol, and the use of the imagination to cross over into God's world—the world of intuition, sacred hunches, and dreams. Jesus then becomes the "icon" and the pathfinder to such a world. His words in Scripture, his Spirit, his energy, and his focus upon ministry provide the bridge to one's inner world and to God's Spirit.

Imagine yourself at the wedding at Cana, described in John 2:1–11. Recall your own celebratory feelings evoked by family weddings. When read with imagination, the story of the wedding at Cana comes alive with delicious scents and the sounds of laughter, music, and merriment. Imagine Jesus, relaxing with friends, caught up in the moment. Get a sense of the crowd. Will his growing celebrity status be a distraction, stealing focus from the wedding party? Was Jesus hoping to maintain a low profile when his mother interrupted his conversation with the urgent request, "Do something; they've run out of wine!" Jesus rises to the occasion: he turns the water into wine. Only the servants know of the miracle. What gives the story interest is the twist at the end, inviting us to use our own imaginations. We smile as the governor of the feast enjoys the wine and marvels that the best has been saved for last.

Imagine, if you will, a modern-day situation: a once active, vibrant church has fallen on hard times. Internal conflict has caused a third of the congregation to leave. The session is faced with a rising debt that has grown to over a million dollars. The budget is tight, with no funds for extras. This was the situation in my church. Enter Advent, the busiest season of the year.

After much discussion, and some dissension, the Session approves a modest mission project to Honduras. They adjourn with a nagging concern about the payment of bills, particularly the winter heating bill.

Fast forward to Sunday morning. The church service is about to begin. Someone enters down the aisle, pushing a red wheelbarrow, nonchalantly parking it in front of the communion table. Nothing is said.

During the offertory, the congregation was asked to give their change to the Honduras Food for Kids project, described as a "meal on wheels" project with no overhead. All of the proceeds would buy food for the children.

There was just one catch: the plate would not be passed around. The parishioners had to walk to the communion table and put their offering into the wheelbarrow! It was all a little silly, and there was a foolish feeling in proposing the idea. Some wondered who thought of the gimmick. Yet each Sunday of Advent, the little, red wheelbarrow maintained its post.

First the kids brought their pennies, and then the parents and grandparents contributed. Soon the idea caught everyone's imaginations. The little, red wheelbarrow seemed to capture the essence of the Christmas spirit. One person realized he had saved his change in the top drawer of his dresser, accumulating over $100.00. He cheerfully gave it all. Soon dollar bills followed the change, attitudes improved, and miracles occurred. Trust was reestablished. The programs were renewed. Finances were stabilized. The million-dollar loan was underwritten. Serious involvement was regained. Change began with a little, red wheelbarrow. Imagination captured God's Spirit and a kind of foolish expectation turned a whole church around.

That is not the end of the story. In November, St. Andrew's Festival was celebrated in "old world" fashion, with bag-pipers, dancers, high liturgy, and communion. Many re-affirmed their baptismal vows.

Mid-winter, a dormant dogwood tree appeared next to the communion table. A note invited worshippers to hang confessions and petitions on its limbs. Spring was still months away, but the little tree began to sprout leaves. This surprised the congregation and brought smiles to many faces. In the collective imagination, a miracle had occurred and God was smiling. The practical person said, "It was the warm air from the furnace that triggered the sap to rise and green leaves to appear." Yes, those winter heating bills had been paid. But the communal spirit in my church was warmed by imagination and the wonder of creation.

There was more to come in the tapestry of the congregational life. A large, blank canvas was erected beside the communion table. Each Sunday, enclosed in the bulletins were strips of ribbon. During communion, the worshippers were encouraged to pin their ribbons on the blank canvas to symbolize their words of thanksgiving, individual prayer requests, and commitments of renewal. A group met later to weave the colorful ribbons into a cross that slowly evolved during the Lenten season. This symbolic, communal gesture evoked in the congregation a paradoxical mix of reverent gentleness and vibrant expectation. What could account for this movement of the Spirit? Creative God, was that your laughter we heard?

We had no official drama team at our church. What a blessing that proved to be. Soon members with a little theater training began to direct aspects of worship. Losing themselves in improvisational play, they introduced props like symbolic stones, keys to the kingdom, and the shepherd's staff. Their childlike spirits refreshed and renewed the services.

The communion table and lectern became a lightning rod for activity. Fine art was projected on a screen to capture the Scripture lessons and sermon topics. Psalms set to music echoed the written Word. We chanted the liturgy and danced the sacred music. Since that remarkable day when we walked up the aisles to deposit change in a little, red wheelbarrow, our lives were never the same. Everything centered around the community table, and we were never again bound, as one parishioner said, by our "pews and cues."

We witnessed the link between symbols, imagination, and emotions. Much preparation went into the planning of these events. There was a lot of perspiration behind the inspiration. Yet, I often felt as if I was in the midst of an interpretive dance. While the worship team worked hard to cover content and maintain focus, there was always room for creativity, for departing from the plan.

No one can say for sure just what effect our imagination had on the restoration of this church congregation, but I am convinced that imagination, focused on the life of Christ, illuminated his humanity and helped us get in step with his teachings.

Henry Nouwen, in *The Only Necessary Thing*, had much to contribute on the subject of imagination. To image or imagine the life of Jesus is to observe his life as it is played out in the Gospels, to catch his humor and resonate with his laughter, to share in his suffering and persecution, to witness his betrayal and the bitter agony of the cross, and to celebrate his ultimate spiritual victory over darkness. Through imagination, we relate to his suffering and make it our own as we face hardships in our own lives. Who has not known disappointment, rejection, betrayal, physical pain, or inconsolable grief? When Christ's words are sacredly kept, we act in more loving and reconciliatory ways. His style becomes ours. He becomes the image, the source of whose we are, and the picture of who we are becoming. Amen!

The ultimate use of image for the church is found in the figure of Christ. Perhaps the mystery of the Eucharist lies in this as well: the breaking of the bread, the pouring of the wine, the words of the sacrament, and the blessing all seem to bring the essence of faith together. Are these symbols indicative of a greater cosmic struggle? Perhaps! At the very least, they point to a drastic schism between the good we perceive in the body of Christ and the evil we encounter in aspects of secular culture. I suggest the ultimate victory, the *Christus Victus* (Latin for *Christ is the Victory*), is found in the image of Christ reflected in us (Nouwen, p. 112–114).

The Imaginative Prototype in Biblical Sources

The final use of imagination is perhaps the most difficult to describe—the prototype of the image of God in man. Again, there is biblical precedence for this source of imagining both in the Old and New Testaments.

So God created human kind [Adam]
In his image
In the image of God
He created them
Male and female
He created them.

—Genesis 1:21–27

When God created human kind [Adam and Eve]
He made them (human)
In the likeness of God
Male and female
He created them
And He blessed them
And named them.
Human kind [Adam and Eve]
When they were created.

—Genesis 5:1–3

Whoever sheds
the blood of a human
By a human shall that person's
Blood be shed
For in his own image
God made humankind.

—Genesis 9:1–7

For man ought not to have
His head veiled
Since he is the image
and reflection of God.

—1 Corinthians 11:7

With it [the tongue] we bless the
Lord and Father
And with it [the tongue] we curse those
who are made
in the likeness of God.

—James 3:9

The use of the "image of God" in the Old Testament references addresses man created in the "image of God." The Old Testament writers' resemblances were concrete, practical, and pictorial. The biblical figures came alive, and contemplation was focused upon life situations and conflicts. The secular and the sacred were interconnected. The world was an expression of the divine personality. Hence God spoke and lived anthropomorphically. He experienced faith in terms of experience. His images took the form of his speaking and hearing, his working and interacting as family. God was the Father. Thus, in Psalm 8, man is granted a status a little less than divine. He rules with glory and the image of God in him is a gift to accomplish his life's purpose (Porteous, p. 682).

The only two passages in the New Testament where the "image of God" appears are 1 Corinthians 11:7 and James 3:9. Both the Hebrew and the Greek translations imply more than image in the sense of likeness or "prototype." It is at this point the New Testament brings the transformation from an image to "the new prototype." The thought of Old Testament man being created in the image of God is now replaced with the thought of Christ as being the image of God, the ultimate divine prototype.

It seems such analyses can only be validated by the method of imagination to grasp their power and insight. One could find support from St. John's writings, and certainly St. Paul's, as they both use the image of Christ as the image of God. But it is the transformation of the idea that grasps the imagination and the power of its truth.

The Johannine Writings

The change of the "image of God in man" to the perfect prototype is not only determinative but also mind stretching. To think that the "image of God in man" was to be replaced with the thought of Christ as the "image of God" and the new divine prototype was profound (Porteous p. 684). But this was precisely the central thrust of Johannine writings and the Apostle Paul's preaching. In Christ, the Lord and Father of the Old Testament becomes visible as the "only Son from the Father," writes John

(John 1:14); when one sees Christ, one knows the Father (John 12:45; 14:9). The Johannine Epistles build on this theme with the category of "the children of God." Believers are like Christ, the divine prototype, in that they become the new divine prototypes for the first generation after Christ. They become the model for the Christian community (1 John 3.2). The creator God becomes visible in the children of God, just as God was visible in Christ. The determinative was abiding in Christ's Spirit and following his example and words. It was a kind of "mystical abiding" that bridges the cultural world and the supernatural. Thus, the cornerstone of the theological world was completely reshaped and developed into the foundation of the church as we know it today.

The Pauline Writings

As noted, St. Paul developed the concept of the "divine prototype" in greater detail as well as the purpose of the church to proclaim the motif of Christ's relationship to the children of light. "He (Christ) is the image of the invisible God, the first-born of all creation, for in him all things were created, in heaven and on earth, visible and invisible, whether thrones or dominion or principalities or authorities—all things were created through him and for him. He is the head of the body, the church" (Col. 1:15–18).

To the Corinthian community, the apostle argues in the same vein, in the light of Jesus' gospel and his own experience of Jesus on the Damascus Road, that the likeness of God is revealed in Christ (2 Cor. 4:4). No doubt the vision of Jesus and the confrontation he perceived conditioned his conviction. Not only was it Jesus' gospel but also the mystical encounter that changed the Apostle (Acts 9:1–88).

In more depth, St. Paul contrasts what he calls the first Adam (humanity) and the second Adam from heaven (Jesus Christ): "Now the Lord is 'the Spirit,' and where the Spirit of the Lord is, there is freedom. And we all, with unveiled face, reflecting the glory of the Lord, are being changed into his likeness from one degree of glory to another; for this comes from the Lord who is Spirit" (2 Cor. 3:17–18).

What is involved in the "unveiled face" is the image of Jesus Christ, as well as the words of Jesus, either sensed intuitively, heard audibly, or conveyed by the Spirit of the Lord. Jesus Christ thus becomes the "new prototype." It is only in relationship to him that the veil can be removed. St. Paul's mind is filled with the thought that "only in relationship to Christ" can mankind find the likeness of God and his power to be changed. Jesus Christ not only becomes the model and the image of God but also the means to the unveiling of God.

Chapter 15

Grace to Service

Serving as a parish minister in the midst of today's culture creates a familiar predicament with regard to church unity and raises two questions that have plagued the church since its early days in Corinth. When does the search for unity go too far? And when does the search for unity fail to go far enough? I am choosing to answer these questions in the best way I can—autobiographically.

My answers are rooted in John's gospel, with Jesus' prayer of consecration (John 17). The cultural setting is filled with conflict and persecution. Jesus, with his enemies closing in, faces betrayal, capture, and crucifixion. He prays that the unity he enjoys with his Father will be extended to his disciples and to those who will follow his teachings. He prays for the disciples' sanctification, that they will become one with him and one with the Father. He prays that the oneness of his relationship with his Father will be mirrored in them and that this oneness will translate to his followers, providing evidence of their oneness with one another and with God.

Herman Thurman, in "We Are One," published in *Weavings*, suggests that the Spirit of God is the unifying force of all life. Responsibility to one's family, to one's neighbor, and to one's community is directly connected to "the Solitary Contemplation of God." For example, we observe the level of unity in a marriage. When harmony is lost, we immediately perceive discord. Thurman explains, "When I have lost harmony with another, my whole life is thrown out of tune. God tends to be remote and far away when a desert and sea appears between me and another. I draw close to God as I draw close to my fellows. The great incentive remains ever alert. I cannot be at peace without God and I cannot be truly aware of God if I am not at peace with my fellows" (p. 16).

The dilemma is clear. Ministry, to remain faithful, requires the search for unity whatever the cost or the difficulty faced. Love and grace are determinative principles of the Jesus Spirit! We would like to dodge or ignore such an injunction, but it is always in the center of Jesus' preaching and is central to the early community's power and influence. It is also relevant for the present, where the gospel is preached and the sacraments are rightly administrated. *Grace* is as an operative word—an energy that is more frequently occurring than we realize. Thus, unity is the characteristic of the paradigm shift and desperately needed in the contemporary community.

Where it All Began: Grace to Service, a Living Paradigm

The poem "I am a Country Boy," found in the introductory pages of this book, describes my ministerial call. I grew up in the country, and I love everything that it represents. In my young mind, a call to ministry, was inconceivable, an absurd idea. The Whippier Will Valley of the American South, the locust singing in the summer, and the rhythm of the seasons filled my boyhood with adventure and variety. Surely God had made a mistake in his selection process, I reasoned upon first sensing the call. The country coursed through my blood and filled my psyche. The winding roads, the pine and oak trees—everything in the environment danced to a music found only in the country.

In the center of my life sat God's church, nestled comfortably beside a beautiful lake. Reverend Autrey, God's man, served in this setting of all that was beautiful. On sultry summer days, we would meet for an all-day songfest and dinner on the tree-laced grounds. We enjoyed a festival of music, food, and storytelling. The lake, called Bay Springs, was fed by a freshwater stream, running deep under the Woodsen Ridge Mountains. Families relaxed in the cool mountain air, and teenagers swam freely in the lake's clear, sparkling waters. The spirit of the place touched the body and soul, especially when the country girls arrived. It was a dynamic and harmonious center nurtured by parents, grandparents, aunts, and uncles, and led by Brother Autrey, as the southern folks called the pastor of the little church. His sermons were stories that were made clear by his deeply-felt spirituality and personal experience of God's grace. His humanity captured my mind and heart; his mistakes and failings were key elements in his Sunday messages. His divorce, uncommon in those days, told the tragic story of love lost, while his six children provided lively examples of God's blessings. His new car, a gift from the parishes, reflected the community's love and devotion to their spiritual leader and friend.

In southern tradition, storytelling was elevated to an art form by authors such as Mark Twain and William Faulkner. To my young ears, these greats met their equal in Autrey's sermons. Autrey wrote too, frequently publishing his work in magazines read throughout the South. As a boy, I listened. I found direction and words that came alive. *If Autrey found forgiveness, perhaps there is a place for this country boy,* I thought. Grace was needed, and Autrey was a model to follow.

The southern society and culture modeled hospitality and friendship to one's neighbors. Families were large; everyone was related. Arguments and strife were common, but always tempered. When tragedy did occur, neighbors arrived to lend a hand. Sometimes folks would forget to be hospitable, but Autrey was quick to remind them. Like the Celts of Scotland, they were spiritually rooted, grounded in nature, and bathed in a culture of hospitality and grace.

We were dependent on the weather and the crops we grew. We paid attention when thunder sounded and lightening flashed. Dark clouds and sudden winds conveyed God's passing visit. We tended to keep life in order, lest God should speak loudly.

I once tried to box God into a corner. I prayed for rain after a particularly long dry spell. The crops were battered and parched by the heat and needed water. It seemed the right thing to do to ask God for help. After all, Autrey's sermon based on Matthew 7:7–8 suggested as much. I reminded God what Jesus had said as I prayed. I was serious about the prayer. The next thing I noticed, the sky grew dark. *Wow!* I thought, *Autrey's sermon was true.*

God's answer to my request revealed his timely sense of humor. His answer came in the form of hail stones, hammering home the message with more than a hint of sarcasm. He was listening. I tried never to challenge God's dark side or his judgment again. The Celtic God of nature and I were on speaking terms despite my age and my questions concerning the raw deals life sometimes gave me. Frequently, more often than not, he gave me help and a direct word out of nowhere.

Country people valued unity and the efforts to "get along," as they would say. Their churches valued networks. Pastors visited pastors whenever they traveled. Their homes offered open doors of hospitality and places to rest. Folks naturally knew each other and worked effectively to build consensus because they learned to trust each other. It was a relational theology that the North never understood and does not understand, even to the present day. There is something grand about the power of fried chicken, wide varieties of homegrown vegetables, and apple or plum pies from the farm kitchen to bond people together. Civil rights marches and the calls to respect the equality of the races tested this unity, but it was held together by the deep bond of community. We could learn much from these Southern traditions.

Autrey modeled well the need for personal connections. Every Sunday after church, a family was assigned the honor of "hosting the preacher." Chicken was the usual fare, with lima beans or black-eyed peas the norm. There was, of course, always corn bread and peach or berry cobbler. It was an honor to "host the preacher," and Mother considered it a time when Autrey would bring his "magic" to my father. They did like each other, I sensed, but my dad had his religious defenses up most of the time, and Autrey's magic didn't touch my father until much later. They both loved the outdoors, and these occasions were opportunities for swapping stories about running of the hounds, river fishing, and bird hunting. These stories created deep bonding for everyone. And it was this bond that brought Dad back to his creator later in his life.

Country people do move, and we were not the exception. In our case, we moved to the Northwest, but the southern traditions, buried deep in my soul, never really left me. Your honor and your word were central to your identity; trust and friendship were basic—they formed your life. Presenting your tithe to God was a commitment; a bond to God was sacred. It seems simple as I look back, those handshakes with God that were put there by Autrey and a mother who expected me to follow what Autrey said. He was God's man. I was never to forget him.

Marriage in the southern tradition is expected, and family plays a large part; although, the service is informal. I married a beautiful young woman whose energy and love keeps getting deeper every year. I attended college in the Northwest and seminary on the Pacific Coast; both were tough, requiring clear thinking and excellence. At that time, I often identified with Job's suffering; though I never felt his answers measured up. Only after reading Karl Jung's analysis, *Answer to Job*, did I feel vindicated.

Seminary education was competitive, with self-interests often butting heads. Achievement was central, with the expectation of performance in organized and measured thought processes. Missing in seminary was a course on how to love, how to forgive, and how to build friendships. Academic discipline warred with my Celtic traditions.

Then something happened to disturb the peace in the catacombs of the seminary: the civil rights marches and the calls for justice rang out. Life 101 marched into the classroom. A group of seminary classmates answered the call and headed off to Selma, Alabama. It was hard to handle. I chose not to go, but I did give all the money I had ($35.00) to a classmate who played tennis with such power that I felt he could handle anything! His name was John Shaw. Later, I marched against violence and learned the meaning of its significance and the dangers too. What I learned is that faith directs a person's attention toward justice. Injustice cannot be tolerated, either in ourselves or in the church. Prejudice needs to be unmasked in ourselves and identified in our systems. Willful behavior needs to surrender to love and friendship. Oneness or unity requires a kind of willingness to wear another's shoes and walk down the other's path. It is something the church has not done well, nor preached well enough, nor grasped to any depth.

Out of this amalgam of experience and exposure, I graduated and was ordained to be a pastor. I certainly didn't know enough, so I took an associate job in the middle of farm country. It was an 800-member church, asleep in the middle of the country. I was delighted; it was a job, and I was a country boy again. Soon, however, the issues of grape boycotts, farm labor disputes, protesting youth, Vietnam, and poverty rose up. The youth, as you could expect, were equal to the task, using folk masses and their ministries to speak. I was their leader, and it was here that I learned that the course not taught at seminary was: How to Love, How to Forgive, and How to Be One. Frankly, I stumbled into the subject in the midst of a sermon one Sunday, and the impression left me surprised. The imprint was clear: "Go down this path, and I will show you the way." I learned to love, first with those kids and then their parish.

Those early years prepared me for the next journey of faith that covered twenty-two years in one parish. I spent what I call "The Beloved Years" in the same home, the same church, and the same town. I matured in my relationships, my sons grew up, and we all went through the variety of stages life gives. I learned that the local parish is essential. I learned that mission beyond the local church is equally as important. I learned bottom-up management. Responsibility was the key to issues we faced. Most of all, I learned to practice love, to teach by example, and to keep a balance between the parish and family. Therapy helped; forgiveness helped; confession helped; grace helped; and my wife, who allowed me to grow and change, helped. Our sons suffered and gained in the process and are today responsible adults who still love us—maybe because we keep working on our relationships with them!

Through a variety of experiences, the local community began to focus beyond itself to the larger community: the inner city needs, missions overseas, soup kitchens, integration in the schools, and the gambling and drug culture. The mission required financial support but also a substantial time commitment on the part of the membership. We were one of the lead churches and often sacrificed until our giving threatened the cash flow necessary for salaries and operating expenses. Often the parishioners got tired and exhausted and sometimes grumbled—this included me.

But then there would be a surprise, a miracle of sorts, and I would be good for another five years! A friend whose name was Eva inherited a twenty-six-foot sailboat. She handed me the keys one Sunday and said, "Sail it, and send me the bills."

"But I don't know how to sail!" I said.

"Jack Moore will help you," she said.

Those gifts of joy kept me going, along with a great staff and a beautiful congregation. I learned to sail in many directions.

Challenges and opportunities to learn continued in the larger judicatory, where the ministry was more difficult to manage. The bin ripened with unresolved issues. Debate was not always civil or respectful. Trust was often broken and differences tested. Tolerance and efforts to love and appreciate differences were non-existent. Sometimes hidden anger and resentments polarized issues. Conservative and liberal factions became "those people" and "us."

Today's struggles are not new. Church history is full of conflict and discord, but at that time in my ministry, this kind of conflict was new to me, and the judicatory work didn't feel right. When does the search for unity go too far? For me, the answer was to drop out of the larger judicatory ministries, only to return later in a call to a new parish and a fresh start at creating oneness.

At this point in my career, opportunities developed that helped to open and make bridges between factions within the new judicatory. I was asked to chair a Presbytery study group to lead the judicatory on the subject of the ordination of gay and lesbian people. We spent a year in the preparation for a two-day conference. It was well planned, staffed, and organized. Small groups were led by team members. New Testament scholars from western seminaries were asked to speak. Medical scholars made presentations. Theologians contributed. It was well attended. Positions on both sides of the aisle didn't change, but they softened. There was more laughter and less anger. In the end, my efforts were acknowledged with a standing ovation. Oneness prevailed, despite the polarized opinions. We knew a lot more about the subject and each other.

Did the search for unity fail to go far enough? The answer is "yes." We could have done more. However, in all fairness, we had also suffered the race riots, school shootings, marches against violence, and a massive earthquake that leveled some of our churches and damaged others. Still, a solidarity or oneness held us together. I was proud to be the moderator of that Presbytery.

Other Areas of Grace

I have a need to share three equally important contexts of grace that resulted in service and paradigm shifts of note. The first was my military service. I was active duty in the Navy and was stationed on carriers for four years. Then I served as a reserve chaplain for twenty-two years, leading a parish and a community as it faced issues of crime, education, and race. How does one frame the place of a chaplain who lives in culture? The answer is simple but difficult to practice. He or she is a guide to God's grace, mercy, and holy presence. Chaplains stand together in their attempts to be guides, whether Catholic or Protestant. The fraternity is close. The unity is based upon respect and friendship. Their focus is upon working together for the good they serve in ministry. They identify with the people they serve. It takes training to understand religious diversity, particularly in the military, but it is also a cultural issue in communities. People perceive religious truth and identification divergently.

In war, the chaplain is a priest, counselor, and advocate of mercy, grace, and the holy. He is the witness of God's compassion and forgiveness. He, like the medical doctor, provides help to the injured and dying. It is here that ecclesiastical differences are overcome, and this ideal of unity is essential to God's ministry.

Naval personnel are highly trained. They live in a dangerous theater, whether aboard ship or engaged in land combat. What is not easily perceived is the hunger and desire to know God. Church call, signaling that religious services are about to begin, is not taken lightly when one is engaged in combat or standing ready in flight quarters. The context is clear. Everyone makes his peace. Everyone prays formally or privately. It is a profound place and time. Differences fall away, and bonds are created. Grace is given. The chaplain serves; although, he may not observe the impact of the Holy presence in his service. In either case, it is profoundly rewarding.

The second context of grace in service was found in "the group." The group was connected to a variety of people who worked on their lives in a therapeutic setting. We met once a week for two hours. We faced the issues of our professions, families, and personal relationships. The leader was a psychotherapist. The context was one of honesty, trust, and truth. Forgiveness and laughter, tears and anxiety were equally a part of "the group." It was hard, complex work. The insights often took time. Confession and regret became avenues to restoration. Love and confrontation resulted in finding truth and freedom. The imprint upon the membership was profound. The experience lived as a grace that brought unity of purpose and service. It was like a good family that accepts, forgives, and loves.

The third vehicle of grace was discovered as a consultant-pastor-priest in two deeply conflicted churches. I had just retired and was restless. I still had a lot of energy and decided to move to the Northwest. The opportunity arose to help a struggling congregation. The assignment looked easy, but it became clear that the work would be difficult. In this context, I found a strange phenomenon that was impossible to identify except to call it evil and its effects manifestations of evil. Evil often hides itself in righteous behavior and arrogance. It clothes itself in lies and confusions. It slanders and seeks to control. Like a virus ignored, its growth infects relationships of faith and friendship. Evil takes form in a variety of ways. Usually it attacks leadership, formal and informal. Disunity is the result. Prayer and meditation, a committed laity, and biblical preaching were the principle defenses to the attacks. Pastors are usually the targets. Lay leaders are equally troubled, because little is understood and known about evil in the modern context. Three years later, the church was restored.

The next context was found in a large community church. The pastor had been asked to resign; there was grief and anger. Discord and disunity were commonly observed. A third of the congregation exited with the departure of the pastor. It took several years for trust to be restored. Missions and levels of service were faced. Dysfunction was identified. The primary problems lay in organizational breakdowns and broken trust. Slowly, unity was achieved as the issues were faced and addressed. Grace was hidden, but it showed itself as the people began to serve and re-own the church and its ministry. Unity and renewed trust were essential. It was a remarkable turn-around. Imaginative worship, a mission to Honduras, the addition of new staff members, and an excited laity, empowered by God's energy, resulted. Renewed vision and mission enabled the church to find its identity and resulted in a sense of togetherness. It was my happiest and most challenging ministry. The memory is fondly kept and the reward profoundly enjoyed.

We are one when we search for harmony. But accord is never easy as we contend with issues and search for truth and the applications of truth. I am convinced that grace is more active than anyone realizes. It reminds us of God's love, acted out in the journey Jesus made to the cross and beyond. St Paul writes: "So that your words may give grace to those who hear," echo God's comfort and attempt to live in harmony (Eph. 4:29).

I penned the following poem to capture the feelings of God's touch in this extraordinary journey of faith, one that I find profoundly real and rewarding.

Grace

A Crazy, Holy Grace
The journey of faith
Crazy in that it wells up
Out of a kind of darkness
Where pain is found
Worlds collide
And inner thoughts connect.
Holy Grace in that it comes
Unearned
Crazy Grace because it heals
And hallows the place and space
Crazy because Grace is personal and fits
Holy because Grace is often routine
But never stale.
Crazy, Holy Grace
Shows itself in the deepest place
And the deepest places we share.

—Chet B. Gean, 2008

References

Badenoch, Bonnie. 2008. *Being a Brain-Wise Therapist.* New York: W.W. Norton & Company, Inc.

Bechtel, Carol M., editor 2008. *Touching the Altar of God.* Grand Rapids, Michigan: Wm. B. Eerdmans Publishing Co.

Blodgett, Barbara J. 2008. *Lives Entrusted.* Minneapolis: Fortress Press.

Boulton, Matthew Myer. 2008. *God Against Religion: Rethinking Christian Theology Through Worship.* Grand Rapids, Michigan: Wm. B. Eerdman Publishing Co.

Buechner, Frederic. 1992. *Listening to Your Life: Daily Meditations with Frederic Buechner.* New York: Harper Collins Publishers.

Buechner, Frederick. 2006. *Secrets in the Dark.* New York: Harper Collins.

Burch Brown, Frank. 2009. *Inclusive, Yet Discerning: Navigating Worship Artfully.* Grand Rapids, Michigan: Wm. B. Eerdmans Publishing Co.

Congar, Yves. October 21, 2008. "Why stop Short of the full use of the Body's Gifts?" *Weavings.* Christian Century.

DeWaal, Esther. 1997. *The Celtic Way of Prayer.* New York: Image Books.

Delbanco, Andrew W. 1955. *The Death of Satan: How Americans Lost the Sense of Evil*. New York: Farrar, Straus, and Giroux.

Dyrness, William D. 2009. *A Primer on Christian Worship*. Grand Rapids, Michigan: Wm. B. Eerdmans Publishing Co.

Ehrich, Tom. September 1, 2008. "Get Ready to Measure." *The Presbyterian Outlook*.

Fromm, Erich. 1964. *The Heart of Man: Its Genius for Good and Evil*. New York: Harper & Row.

Fant Clyde E., Jr., and William M Pinson, Jr. 1971. *20 Centuries of Great Preaching*. "Paul Tillich." Vol. 10. Waco, Texas: Word Books.

Farhadion, Charles E. 2007. *Christian Worship Word Wide*. Grand Rapids, Michigan: Wm. B. Eerdmans Publishing Co.

Fitzmyer, Joseph A. 1993. *Anchor Bible*. Romans. New York: Doubleday. 33, 641: intro IX.D.

Frank, Robert and Amir Ffrati. June 30, 2009. "Evil Madoff Gets 150 Years in Epic Fraud." *Wall Street Journal CCLIII(No.151)*.

Jung, C.G. 1973. *Answer to Job*. New York: Princeton University Press.

Jung, C.G. 1965. *Memories, Dreams, Reflections*. New York: Vintage Books Edition.

Kahn, Paul W. 2007. *Out of Eden*. Princeton: Princeton University Press.

Kelsey, Morton T. 1977. *Can Christians Be Educated?* Birmingham, Alabama: Religious Education Press Inc.

Kelsey, Morton T. 1978. *Discernment: A Study in Ecstasy and Evil*. New York: Paulist Press Inc.

May, Gerald G. 1982. *Will and Spirit: A Contemplative Psychology*. New York: Harper Collins.

MacLean, Norman. 1992. *Young Men & Fire*. Chicago: The University of Chicago Press.

Muilenburg, James. 1961. *The Way of Israel*. New York: Harper & Row.

Niebuhr, Reinhold. 1944. *Children of Light and Children of Darkness*. New York: Charles Scribner's Sons.

Niebuhr, Reinhold. 1952. *The Irony of American History*. Chicago: University of Chicago Press. *The Progressive Christian*. Nov.–Dec., 2008.

Neibuhr, Reinhold. 1974. Edited by Ursula M. Neibuhr. *Justice and Mercy*. New York: Harper & Row.

Neibuhr, H. Richard. 1951. *Christ and Culture*. New York: Harper & Row.

Norris, Kathleen. March 18, 1998. "Sinatra in the Bell Tower." *Christian Century*. Page 25.

Nouwen, Henri J.M. 1992. *The Return of the Prodigal Son: A Story of Homecoming*. New York: ImageBooks: Doubleday.

Nouwen, Henri. 1999. *The Only Necessary Thing: Living a Prayerful Life*. New York: Crossroad Publishing Co.

Palmer, Parker J. March/April 2009. "The Broken-Open Heart." *Weavings XXIV*(2). Christian Century.

Peterson, Eugene H. Peterson. 2002. *The Message: The Bible in Contemporary Language*. Colorado Springs, CO: Alive Communications.

Plantinga Jr., Cornelius and Sue A. Rozeboom. 2003. *Discerning the Spirits: A Guide to Thinking About Christian Worship Today*. Grand Rapids, Michigan: Wm. B. Eerdman Publishing Co.

Porteous, N.W. 1962. *The Interpreter's Dictionary*. Nashville: Abingdon Press.

Rediger, I. G. 1997. *Clergy Killers*. Louisville, Kentucky: Westminster John Knox Press.

Sittler, Joseph A. 1981. *Grace Notes, and other Fragments*. Philadelphia: Fortress Press.

Taylor, Jill Bolte, Ph.D. 2006. *My Stroke of Insight*. New York: Viking.

Thurman, Herman. "We Are One." *Weavings XXIII*(3). *Page 16*.

Tillich, Paul. 1971. *20 Centuries of Great Preaching*. Waco, Texas: Word Books Publisher.

Trachtman, Paul. January, 2009. "Night Visions." *Smithsonian Magazine*. Page 68–73.

Waetjen, Herman C. 2005. *The Gospel of the Beloved Disciple*. New York: T & T Clark.

Vischer, Lukas, editor. 2003. *Christian Worship in Reformed Churches Past and Present*. Grand Rapids, Michigan: Wm. B. Eerdmans Publishing Co.

Winters, Bradford. 2008. "A Conversation with Walter Brueggemann." *Image Journal* (55). Retrieved from http://www.imagejournal.org/page/journal/backissues-55.

Winters, Bradford. October 08 Part A. "Interview with Walter Brueggeman." *Context* "Use Your Imagination."

To purchase a signed copy of *Pass the Peace: A New Paradigm for Christian Community*, arrange an author signing, or schedule a speaking engagement, please contact Dr. Gean directly by email, <u>chetgean@msn.com</u>, or phone: (253) 225-0624.

WinePressPublishing
Great Books, Defined.

To order additional copies of this book call:
1-877-421-READ (7323)
or please visit our website at
www.WinePressbooks.com

Dr. Chet Gean earned a Bachelors of Arts from Whitworth College. He graduated from San Francisco Theological Seminary, completing a Masters of Divinity and Doctorate of Ministry. He served twenty-six years of active and reserve duty as a naval chaplain. For many years he was the pastor at Calvary Presbyterian Church at Hawthorn California and also served at Kirk O' the  Valley Presbyterian Church in Reseda, CA. Most recently he has worked as an interim pastor for conflicted churches in the Seattle area. With the publishing of *Pass the Peace*, Chet sets sail in a new direction. In the wake of his parish experience, Dr. Gean identifies the challenges and opportunities facing the church today, and charts a new course for Christian community.

CPSIA information can be obtained at www.ICGtesting.com
Printed in the USA
BVOW032345041212

307297BV00001B/27/P